Birds on the Couch

Birds on the Couch

The Bird Shrink's Guide to Keeping Polly from Going Crackers and You Out of the Cuckoo's Nest

RUTH HANESSIAN
WITH WENDY BOUNDS

Crown Publishers, Inc./New York

Note: Many of the names and identifying details in this book have been changed to protect the privacy of the birds.

Published by Crown Publishers, Inc., 201 East 50th Street, New York, New York 10022. Member of the Crown Publishing Group.

Random House, Inc. New York, Toronto, London, Sydney, Auckland
www.randomhouse.com

CROWN and colophon are trademarks of Crown Publishers, Inc.

Printed in the United States of America

Design by LYNNE AMFT

Illustrations by PAULA COHEN

Library of Congress Cataloging-in-Publication Data

Hanessian, Ruth.
Birds on the couch : the bird shrink's guide to keeping Polly from going crackers and you out of the cuckoo's nest / by Ruth Hanessian with Wendy Bounds. —1st ed.
1. Cage birds—Behavior—Anecdotes. 2. Cage birds—Training—Anecdotes. 3. Hanessian, Ruth. I. Bounds, Wendy. II. Title.
SF461.6.H35 1998
636.6'8—dc21 98-6118

ISBN 0-609-60239-X

10 9 8 7 6 5 4 3 2 1

First Edition

To Bill, my cockatoo—the first big bird I ever owned, and the smartest.

Contents

~~~~~~~~~~~~~~~~~~~~~~~~~~~~~~

Acknowledgments

First and foremost, I want to thank the birds.

They are the ones, of course, who have made these wonderful tales possible and provided me and so many others with joy and companionship. And special gratitude goes to all the people who love birds, particularly my friend and customer Barbara McConagha, who first helped me bring these stories to light by helping alert *People* magazine to my tales. To everyone at Animal Exchange, both my customers and my faithful staff—thank you for your support and dedication to these pets and this project.

To Sue Carswell, the dynamic editor who spied the bird from afar, so to speak, and made this book happen. Thank you, Sue, for introducing me to Wendy Bounds, the writer who fashioned my scattered thoughts into a cage for birds and did not mind that I worked with a pencil and not a typewriter.

Finally, my dearest love and thanks to my wonderful mother and my three children, all of whom have always enjoyed and respected pet birds and have helped me constantly through life.

The Old Man and the Bird

All animals are equal, but some animals are more equal than others.

—GEORGE ORWELL, *ANIMAL FARM*

PEOPLE OFTEN ASK ME WHY I'VE DE-voted half of my fifty-eight years to working with pet birds. I usually answer by recounting the story of Mr. Reed.

We first met in the early 1980s. Back then Mr. Reed was like many of the elderly people I encountered in nursing homes and senior citizen residences near Animal Exchange, my Rockville, Maryland, pet store. The Great Depression had stripped Mr. Reed early in life not only of his money and pride but also of his ability to trust in mankind. As far as I knew, he had never married, he had no children, and after four decades of isolation in different institutions, he was withdrawn and uncommunicative.

Now in his eighties, Mr. Reed hid his loneliness behind thick black-rimmed glasses that dwarfed his weathered blue eyes. He shuffled about inside the quiet nursing home, unwilling to smile or converse with anyone. Mr. Reed's only companions, it seemed to me, were whatever memories he kept to himself.

That all changed one crisp autumn morning. Despite his aloofness, Mr. Reed was quite interested in the activities going on in the nursing home lobby. On this particular day I arrived from Animal Exchange with a pair of gregarious green lovebirds. They were about five inches long, chunky in stature, with blue rumps and bright peach-colored foreheads.

Through my involvement with a group called People Animals Love (PAL), I was scheduled to deliver the two love-birds for placement inside this nursing home's lobby, where I hoped they would enliven the sterile surroundings. PAL was a nonprofit program created to link animals with people who lived in institutions such as nursing homes, senior residences, and prisons. Although each institution's staff was officially responsible for the care of the animals, lonesome patients looking for companionship often assumed the feeding and other responsibilities themselves. Birds made particularly suitable pets in such locations because they stayed caged, were often chatty, and could eat almost any type of people food without fear of upset tummies. Looking after the birds often instilled a sense of purpose in these patients' otherwise monotonous lives. As for the birds, they were blessed with attentive care from people who had few other obligations.

That fall day I situated the pair of lovebirds in a semicircular silver cage, which I hung against a wall next to a fading picture of the home's rather stern-looking founder. Underneath the cage I placed a small book about their care. The barren, medicinal-smelling lobby quickly warmed with the delightful sound of their chirping and wing-flapping.

Seniors passed by with their walkers and canes, peering at the creatures. Although a few residents seemed wary, most could barely conceal their curiosity, pointing wrinkled fingers at the cage and grinning when the birds jumped about.

Mr. Reed, meanwhile, circled the room nervously, keeping to himself and trying to conceal his interest in the excited lovebirds. Finally, after the room cleared out for lunch, he stopped directly beside their cage. Glancing to see who was watching, he picked up the bird book, eased into a nearby chair, and began reading. For hours he remained by the birds' side, studiously examining the guide.

When my day's visit ended, I approached him cautiously. "Would you like to help take care of these birds for a few days?" I asked. He looked up, his dulled eyes flickering behind his glasses. Then he nodded, a tiny tentative smile creeping onto his lips.

As the weeks progressed, I learned from the nursing home staff that Mr. Reed had gradually assumed all the care and feeding of the lovebirds. One morning I received a call from the home saying Mr. Reed felt the birds were ready to mate. I drove over to check, and indeed, Mr. Reed's diagnosis was correct—it seems he'd learned a great deal from studying the little book I'd left behind. Together, Mr. Reed and I offered the lovebirds a small wooden box, which they gladly accepted and began filling with shredded newspaper and other materials to create a nest. Throughout the afternoon, as Mr. Reed watched protectively, the carefree birds sang love songs and bustled about constructing a fine crib for their eggs.

A few days later I stopped by to appraise the lovebirds' progress and noticed a very odd white and brown material lining the nest.

"What a strange-looking nest, Mr. Reed," I noted. "Do you mind my asking what's in there?"

"Toast," he replied in a proud voice. "Every morning I save a piece of my breakfast toast for the birds. They seem to like it."

I nodded and marveled at the profound change in this man. Not long ago he had been tired and reclusive; now he interacted regularly with the staff while caring for these love-birds with the devotion of a conscientious innkeeper. Watching them eat and nest, he would chuckle as they bobbed their heads about, dancing as if they knew it brought him plea-sure. After years of speaking only when spoken to, Mr. Reed would invite other residents to witness the lovebirds' antics.

These creatures, I realized, had become much more than transient boarders passing through Mr. Reed's life. If their relationship had begun as tenant and landlord, the birds and Mr. Reed were now each other's only family. Through some mutual agreement struck gradually over mornings of shared breakfast and evenings of simple conversation, the birds had decided to keep Mr. Reed, and he in turn agreed to spend his remaining years with them. It seemed a fair bargain.

Soon the lovebirds produced two charming babies whom we moved into Mr. Reed's room, along with their mother and father. The babies also attached themselves to Mr. Reed, and we trimmed their wing feathers so they could venture outside their cage to interact with him. To this day I keep a picture in my store of the little lovebirds cuddling beneath the crisp collar of Mr. Reed's shirt, their green heads peeking out to rest on his fuzzy black cardigan.

Several times I saw him gently placing one of the baby birds in the trembling hands of other senior citizens, assuring them that the birds would cause no harm. Every Sunday there was at least one resident whose family would fail to show up for a visit as promised. Mr. Reed always made certain the lovebirds spent extra time cuddling in the arms of that senior. In many ways Mr. Reed became the center of social activity at the home.

One winter evening, after a pleasant dinner with his chattering family, Mr. Reed went to bed, as usual, at nine o'clock. The next morning, when the lovebirds cried for his attention, he did not wake up. Sometime in the predawn hours, Mr. Reed had died in his sleep. The two baby birds and their parents tried to rouse him throughout the morning, but eventually quieted as they watched the nursing home staff strip Mr. Reed's now empty bed. Perhaps they understood what had happened. I never underestimate an animal's capacity to comprehend the human world.

Mr. Reed's story stays with me as a reminder of the power these winged creatures have to improve the quality of human lives. They can talk, providing companionship to the lonely. They can share meals, nibbling a bit of hamburger bun or a morsel of home-cooked fried chicken. They can chatter in the shower, serve as an excellent alarm clock, or sit on your shoulder as you fold laundry. They never need to take a walk. They are good listeners and, as I personally discovered, attentive nursemaids.

While I was recovering from breast cancer in 1993, a tiny green kakariki bird with a lovely red forehead and a long, streaming tail rested patiently on the couch with me. Those were not my finest days. Fatigue from chemotherapy had left me too exhausted to work or even carry on an extended conversation with my human friends. But Katie, as I called her, was different. She was content to while away the hours reading over my shoulder or watching *60 Minutes.* Katie didn't look at me any differently when I lost my hair or when I was too weak to bathe. After my surgery I stayed at home alone for nearly two weeks. Sometimes I could summon the energy to work on a jigsaw puzzle. Katie was always there to watch my progress, sometimes picking up pieces of the puzzle herself and dropping them on the floor. Granted, this often slowed down the completion of the project, but I didn't mind. Truly, I was grateful for any companion who didn't require me to be cheerful and alert.

When I first returned to work at the store, I could gather only enough strength to stay for a few hours each day, and even then I wasn't much help to my staff. My relationship with others seemed cloudy as they tiptoed around, taking care not to trouble me with too many details. But at home with Katie, nothing changed. She constantly amused me by climbing up the curtains, hiding her little eight-inch body under the sofa, and burrowing her head in my neck when I shut my eyes for a brief nap.

Throughout my recovery, Katie and I ate together, listened to bluegrass tunes together, and often prayed together. I lived alone, and other family members came and went, their attention dictated by busy life schedules that didn't disappear just because I was sick. But Katie willingly adjusted her routines—her morning bath, her midday romp with her toy rings, and even her early bedtime—to fit my schedule. When I felt too nauseated or weak to eat, Katie would stand by, refusing to feast on her tiny granules of birdseed until I took at least one bite of scrambled eggs. If I lay still for too long, she might whistle a bit in my direction, just to remind me that she was in the room and watching over me.

My recuperation was slow but successful. When I think back over the months I spent sluggishly commuting from my house to the doctor and the store—months filled with hours when I confronted my fear of death and struggled not to ask pointless questions, like "Why?"—I think sometimes that it was Katie who saved me. I couldn't ignore her vibrant personality and the songs she so readily sang for me. What's more, she still needed and depended on me for food and care. And I know now that our routines, no matter how mundane, were the very threads that kept me tied to the sometimes elusive act of living.

It was during my days at home with Katie that I really took the time to think about how the companionship of birds can be so special and distinct from that of other pets. It was then that the first seed for this book was planted in my head. Much has been written about the endearing and exceptional qualities of dogs and cats, but very little has been said about the delights and challenges of owning pet birds.

In 1982 I started a program called Lend-a-Pet at the Rockville Senior Center in Maryland. The birds involved were unwanted, turned over to my store by owners who could no longer care for them. Some of the birds had obvious quirks. Others seemed perfectly normal. But all were in need of love and companionship.

My hope with the program was to play matchmaker and give these senior citizens a focus beyond their next meal or medication dosage. When seniors took a liking to a bird, we'd "lend" them that bird to take home for a month, instructing them carefully on proper care. Most chose to keep the birds beyond the month, but we always called the relationship a loan, believing the burden of caring for an animal indefinitely was too stressful for people who were worried about their own health.

We realized that many of the seniors, already in their late eighties and early nineties, might not outlive the birds they adopted. But for a time the pets brought them merriment. And the new proud parents would return to the senior center on the first Wednesday of each month, laughing and prattling about the escapades of their birds. Their stories and frustrations sounded remarkably similar to the sentiments expressed by the hundreds of customers who came into my store every month to bombard me with questions:

> Why does my bird swear like a sailor?
> Why does he torment the cat by calling her in my
> voice?
> Why can't my bird sleep past 6:30 A.M. on
> Saturdays?
> Why does my bird insist on eating her droppings?
> Why does Fred rub on my finger and leave a wet
> spot? (Trust me, it's a sign of love.)
> Why does he insist on biting the hand that feeds
> him?

As I guided and coached these bird lovers through their various avian crises it became clear that what makes birds so special and endearing is often the same thing that makes them so peculiar. Their voices, their beaks, their wings, can easily lead them to mischief and they will behave in complex, often baffling ways that aren't shared by other domesticated pets. Birds have distinct personalities, and sometimes their actions can—how shall we say it?—drive their owners a little cuckoo. Over and over I heard senior citizens and my customers say insistently, "Ruth, I think my bird is crazy. Listen to what he did. . . ."

The more I listened to their tales, the clearer it became that the owner, more often than not, was actually encouraging the bird's undesirable behavior. In other words, the owners—no matter how well intentioned—were acting in a manner that actually reinforced a bird's deviant actions.

For example, humans can unwittingly encourage their bird to spew blasphemies or to shovel food onto the carpet. They can create an environment in which the bird has no choice but to bite or fly headfirst into a windowpane. When told of these mishaps, I would assure owners that their bird wasn't wacko. Then I would explain why I believed Polly was acting a particular way and suggest ways to control her actions. Often this meant recommending that my customers change some aspect of their own treatment of Polly.

Since I heard the same tales from many people, it didn't take me long to realize that most bird owners could benefit from a little Bird Psychology 101. I started teaching regular classes in parrot psychology at the store, coaching my students on how to cope with their birds. Like group therapy sessions, these classes gave people a chance to hear how other bird owners dealt with similar problems and to learn what mistakes they were making in caring for their birds.

~~~~~~~

As I recovered from cancer and began to think about writing a book, my recollection of all these stories intrigued and inspired me. While birds, particularly members of the parrot family, are undeniably delightful, they are also very smart. Many even outsmart their owners. Ultimately, that's how *Birds on the Couch* was hatched—as a guide for those who want to enjoy a fruitful, healthy relationship with their particular Polly.

If you have ever fallen victim to your bird's craftiness, perhaps you can benefit from the stories that follow. In each chapter I've tried to bring to light many basic facts—that wet birds don't fly as well as dry ones, for example, and that too much light can make a bird particularly promiscuous—and I encourage you to look for the obvious cause when you analyze the behavior of your own bird.

Birds have the potential to bring us much daily pleasure, to lift our beleaguered spirits, and to offer camaraderie in a way no other pet can. But they will be much more enjoyable pets when we better understand them and no longer let them push us around. So if you adore your Polly but don't understand why she hates your husband, chases your children, or bites your sister's earlobe, don't give up.

The bird shrink is here to help.

CHAPTER 1

Picking the Right Polly:
Does she match the drapes?

Go slow. Stop and think. Don't rush. . . .
Take time to look at the room and decide
what you really want. . . . In my houses, you
can go from room to room and nothing ever
clashes.

—MARTHA STEWART

THE GENTLEMAN WAS ADAMANT.

He wanted the full-grown one-year-old Mexican red-headed Amazon parrot. No other bird would do. Now, granted, this bright green parrot, with her fifteen-inch wingspan, penetrating black eyes, and red forehead, was one of the more magnificent creatures perched in my shop. But Roger, my customer, lived in a small one-bedroom apartment with his wife, and their previous bird experience was limited to a few, unassuming parakeets. Like a restless sports car owner, he wanted to trade up to a bigger bird with more horsepower, so to speak. This isn't always a good idea, particularly when the living quarters are cramped. He assured me that he would be moving into a bigger house soon, and he remained resolute in his determination to own the Mexican red.

I still wasn't convinced this was a wise decision, and I reminded him, as I often must with my male customers, that size isn't all that matters.

A big bird, I warned, might just sit passively, thinking his magnitude would make up for a lack of personality. Or he might holler mightily, demanding attention, and then become gun-shy when his owner approached the cage for a kiss. These things matter in a long-term relationship, and I carefully explained this to Roger.

What about a sensitive masked lovebird? I suggested. Only four inches long with a chic black face and a bright blue body, she might work nicely. Or the serene green Indian ring-necked parakeet with his stunning long tail and the very fashionable ring of dark feathers circling his neck? They were both interesting, docile birds that would make lovely pets.

"No, no," he insisted, shaking his head. Only the Mexican red would suffice. That was what he wanted. And that was the only bird he was going to buy.

Finally I asked Roger outright why he was so stubborn. He fidgeted for a moment, looked around to make certain no one could hear us, and then whispered bashfully, "I used to date a redheaded Mexican named Sabrina."

I sold him the bird.

As unscientific as it seems, Roger's process of selection was on target. The first step to keeping Polly happy is simply to pick the right Polly for you. Therefore it makes sense to find a bird who pleases you from the start. Roger, for example, was more

likely to dote on a bird who evoked fond memories of a passionate tryst than one who didn't. (I don't know what the bird did for his marriage.)

Unfortunately, not all bird buyers are as clearly in touch with their needs and wants as Roger. Often they forget to consider certain important principles when picking a feathered friend. Here are some initial questions I suggest asking yourself before you take the plunge into avian parenthood.

> Can you stand looking at all those awful fluorescent plastic links she loves to hang from?
>
> Does the bird match your curtains?
>
> Will you freak out if Polly screams during dinner parties or deposits droppings on your Oriental carpet?
>
> You could banish her to the bedroom, but what if she learns to mimic your lovemaking cries— particularly when your mother-in-law is visiting?

Trust me, these are real issues. If you aren't satisfied with the way a bird fits into your household, you won't be happy with the bird—and your bird will sense this and react accordingly. I've seen birds lash out at their owners by screaming whenever they approach, rattling their cage doors incessantly, and mercilessly yanking the hair of unsuspecting visitors. These are attention-grabbing actions, and they are usually seen in birds who don't feel they are properly appreciated and worshiped by their owners.

For starters, I recommend you thoroughly question pet store personnel about a bird's individual peculiarities and then think carefully about the environment in which you'll place

Polly. A little homework can save a lot of heartache and disappointment for both bird and owner. Wise shoppers don't buy cars without knowing the mechanics of a particular make and model or where they'll park it when they get home. Careful collectors don't purchase art to display without mulling how well it will blend in with the rest of their collection. And smart bird owners shouldn't recklessly commit themselves to a relationship with a pet before contemplating how the new creature will mesh with all aspects of their home and its current inhabitants.

The following is an informal guide I recommend using when Polly-picking.

FAMILY MATTERS

Do you live with someone?

If so, it's wise to make certain that person will welcome a winged stranger into your house. Like all pets, a bird is an addition to the family. But birds have some special traits that distinguish them from cats, dogs, and fish. They love to stare at themselves in the mirror, for example. They can deliberately hurl food at visitors, and they poop like clockwork when certain members of the family walk into the room. And when they perform in this manner, you cannot put them out in the backyard to cool off, as you might do with other household creatures. A bird, in other words, is a formidable presence. A bird will be noticed.

Consider my friends Susan and Pat. Susan ran a cosmetics telemarketing operation from inside their modest house. A workaholic, Susan was accustomed to placing calls in relative peace under the watchful gaze of the couple's three parakeets.

One day her husband, Pat, hoping to surprise Susan on her birthday, showed up brandishing a garrulous lovebird who already boasted a broad vocabulary. Certainly the dear man meant well. But, alas, the lovebird was so enamored of his new friends, the parakeets, that he couldn't stop chatting.

Susan tried separating the birds in different rooms. But the distance only encouraged the lovebird to raise his voice. Soon it became increasingly difficult for Susan to pitch the merits of cobalt eyeliner and creamy jet-black mascara while the lovebird was shouting at his friends.

"Hello, hello, *hello!*" he would call. "Wanna play with me? *Play with me.*" In turn, the parakeets would chirp back with all the volume they could muster.

When her customers began complaining about the happy squawking, Susan decided that was the final straw. She banished the lovebird to the basement during work hours. Unfortunately for Pat, the basement was a mess, and he was forced to spend Super Bowl Sunday clearing a suitable space for the birthday bird to live.

The next year he chose a juice maker and a nice dinner for Susan's birthday.

Spouses aren't the only family members who should be consulted before a new bird comes home. Is your son old enough to understand that shutting the front door behind him is a must when the bird is outside its cage? If not, you can say good-bye to Caspar the Cockatoo, who will fly out the front door if given the slightest opportunity. More important, if Caspar is fluttering about unattended, can the kids remember to close the toilet seat lid?

I get several calls a year from shocked bird owners who watched Polly spin down the porcelain tube after getting her wings caught in the swirling waters of the commode. How could this happen? Very simply, really. After taking care of business, the owner stands up, flushes, and then realizes too late that a curious Polly has flown in for a closer peek at the exciting swirling activity in the bowl. The suction from the flushing quickly pulls the bird in and either drowns her or sucks her down the tube. I never know how to console those customers who tell me their curious bird has disappeared into the city's sewage system. I think it's a particularly undignified way to go.

THE EARLY BIRD

Naturally, it's impossible to predict the behavior of each individual bird. My daughter Lynn's lovebird, Edgar, was an early riser—not that Lynn knew that when she bought him. Lynn, by comparison, liked to stay in bed past 9:00 A.M. on weekends. Edgar tried mightily to influence her sleep patterns by chirping loudly around 5:30 A.M. Every morning, without fail, he started singing the moment the sun's first rays peeked through the windows. This habit might have proved irreconcilable between them had Lynn not arrived at a clever solution: covering the cage at night with a well-ventilated, thick gold-printed corduroy cloth. It was Lynn's most ambitious sewing project yet. In the darkened atmosphere, dear Edgar was always surprised to discover morning had already arrived when Lynn finally uncovered his cage around 9:15 A.M.

Lynn was imaginative enough to work through her differences with Edgar. And indeed, ingenuity is often the key to handling a bird's quirks.

Lovebirds can be strong and opinionated pets. They demand owners who can tolerate their neediness without becoming pushovers. When my own mother bought her lovebird, Charlie, she discovered he liked to chew shoelaces whenever he was released from his cage. Rather than open her entire closet to his nibbling, she gave him his very own comfortable worn-out walking shoe—an old one that had served Mother well for years. She also cleverly threaded pieces of paper onto the laces for extra chewing fun. Mother held firm, refusing to let Charlie even think about nibbling on any other shoes. Eventually he settled down and obliged. But someone without her patience or creativity might have ended up with a lot of ragged footwear. Heaven forbid if a bird got your Guccis!

To decide what kind of bird is most suitable for your own lifestyle, think first about your daily habits and activities. Do you want a bird who can easily sit on your barbell while you bench-press? In that case think about choosing a petite sun conure. These are bright orange birds with green-and-blue wings and an ebony bill. They are only about thirty centimeters long, and I know a peach-fronted one who adapted well to his owner's exercise ritual and didn't get in the way. By contrast, a giant three-foot-tall blue-and-gold macaw with his large beak and great wingspan might be more distracting than inspirational. His wild flapping during your final repetition probably wouldn't prove conducive to a concentrated workout. And you know, accidents *can* happen. I always say, the bigger the bird, the messier what falls.

Don't dismiss that macaw completely, however. He might be quite suitable for other activities. Some young men hope to impress women when they take their adorable brown Lab puppy for a walk. I've seen the same wishful thinking applied to birds. I know one strapping young man who lets his macaw perch on the handlebars of his motorcycle when he cruises through town. (Please note, this isn't an activity I recommend. Motorcycling is dangerous enough for people, not to mention birds who don't typically wear protective helmets.) The two ride through the park, stopping at crosswalks and eliciting coos and admiring glances from female joggers who are impressed by the handsome bird with his rugged black facial stripes. Sometimes the macaw responds to their attention with phrases he has picked up from his owner. "Pretty girls, pretty girls," he croons. "Nice package, honey. That's a nice package!"

Okay, so tact and subtlety obviously aren't high on this particular guy's bird-training agenda.

Nevertheless, such bold posturing wouldn't work with a smaller bird, who couldn't withstand the wind force of the motorcycle in motion—and wouldn't attract nearly as much attention.

HOME ALONE

In addition to the various activities you'll enjoy with your bird, it's also important to decide how much time you realistically can spend entertaining the creatures. Frequent travelers would do better not to choose a tightly bonded codependent umbrella cockatoo, an all-white bird with a large flat white crest. This bird would truly hate being left alone, and I've known many who grew too despondent to eat or play with their wooden chew blocks and lava rocks when their owners left them for extended periods of time.

You can board your bird at a local pet store when you travel. But if you do, it's wise to check in at least once by telephone to let Polly hear your voice and know you care. This is as much for your well-being as for Polly's. Birdy camp, as I call it, is filled with new experiences and friends, and most owners, particularly new ones, are quite anxious about whether their bird will remember them when they return.

Owners frequently run up their long-distance bills by telephoning Animal Exchange from as far away as Nepal to say good night to their birds. Now, granted, I do feel a little foolish holding my cordless telephone up to a birdcage, particularly when the store is packed with new customers who haven't yet experienced this kind of separation anxiety. But I know that a little babying is also good for Polly who doesn't understand that her owners' frequent flyer miles were about to expire and *that's* why she's spending the night alone in a dark, unfamiliar room with a bunch of noisy strangers who don't respect her privacy. So I always accept traveling customers' phone calls—as long as they're not collect, of course.

HONEY, WAS THAT THE PHONE?

Now, let's say you want a talker. All members of the parrot family *can* talk. Whether they *will* voice their opinions once you get them home is another story. Numerous factors affect a bird's speech patterns, not all of which you can control. Although there are ways to encourage birds to vocalize, I urge you to pick a bird you like regardless of whether it's chatty or silent.

If you do wind up with a conversationalist, make certain you can live with the consequences. A bird can mimic your voice, imitate fire sirens, and parody the mutterings of an ex-spouse with sometimes painful accuracy. Do you really want to continue hearing "Honey, my dinner's cold!" even after the divorce is final?

A bird can taunt your cat or repeat conversations you thought were private. Some birds can accurately imitate the sound of your doorbell, your cellular phone, and your beeper. A bird, in other words, can become annoying. It's unrealistic to expect a bird to limit its vocabulary to "hello" and "I love you" when it hears so many other fine expressions spewing from your mouth. Say no evil and Polly will repeat no evil.

IT'S ALL ABOUT LOCATION

Okay, you've thought your decision through, decided you can't live without that lovely green parakeet, taken the plunge, and bought the bird. Now what? To ensure a new bird's smooth transition into your home, you'll want to figure out exactly where she will live *before* she gets there.

For starters, there's the matter of ambience. Remember how much those new teal-blue draperies cost? Would Martha Stewart approve of the lime green parakeet dangling beside them? If you're thinking of putting Polly in the kitchen, where you eat, think about how her ramblings might sound during the evening's dinner blessing. Perhaps you'll keep her in the study? How will that staid space look with a giant, awkward macaw hanging upside down next to the complete works of James Joyce and Charles Dickens? And keep your beautifully bound books out of the range of his beak, or it won't be long before your library looks as if it's been through a shredder. My hyacinth macaw, Andy, uses his powerful toes to pull folders from my office shelves and scatter them on the floor. Unfortunately he never bothers to put them back.

Andy's actions are by no means unique. In general, birds can be messy. Like restless children, they may think it's fun to dash about their cages, decorating your living room floor with seeds and Polly poop. Don't place decorative objects on top of their cages. I knew one young man who, in preparation for a romantic dinner with his girlfriend, placed a lit candle on top of his spirited bird's cage. During dessert, the antsy bird knocked the candle off the top with a quick jab of his foot, setting the room on fire—and not in the manner that this amorous young man had intended.

Note that your personal space isn't the only concern when bringing a new bird home. If you already own other pets, it's worth weighing their feelings before introducing a new bird into the family. If your cat likes to sprawl on the living room windowsill, don't invite catastrophe by dangling your new Polly overhead. Remember Sylvester and Tweetie? There's a lesson to be learned from that cartoon; why Tweetie's owner perpetually left the bird swinging and singing over Sylvester's kitty bed, I'll never understand. Be sensitive to both pets and place the bird where she won't seem like such a tantalizing treat.

Although it's important for Polly to have one particular place she can call home, some owners like to move their bird from room to room. This is absolutely fine, but in such cases I suggest investing in more than one cage.

That's what the Kylies should have done from the start.

Mr. and Mrs. Kylie were so attached to their yellow parakeet Jefron that they hauled him to their bedroom every night. That meant lugging his large, heavy cage up a long flight of stairs. The husband was an engineer and his wife was an interior decorator. With their combined expertise, I really felt they should have known this arrangement was an accident waiting to happen.

Nevertheless, one night Mrs. Kylie tripped, and Jefron's cage plummeted down the staircase, much like a wooden barrel hurling over Niagara Falls. The cage was collapsible and broke into several pieces when it landed. Miraculously, the stunned bird wasn't hurt—dazed and confused, perhaps, but intact—except for one yellow feather lying on the bottom step.

Because cats are the only creatures fortunate enough to boast nine lives, I figure this bird got lucky, and I *strongly* recommended the Kylies buy an extra cage for their bedroom. They agreed, and Jefron is now much safer riding on the Kylies' shoulders during these evening migrations. If someone trips, the bird can simply glide to a secure landing. I can't vouch for the owners' well-being.

CHICKS WHO'VE BEEN AROUND THE BLOCK

Before nobly opening your home to a "used" bird, take heed. The bird could harbor major behavioral problems that have been reinforced by his previous owner. A newly weaned baby bird from a good source is your best bet. That way, you can control from the beginning what habits the bird picks up. But there are perfectly wonderful previously owned birds in the world that need loving homes and can liven up your household. .

If you fall madly in love with a grown-up bird, ask why the bird needs a new home. Is it because the owner moved into a no-pets apartment? That's a perfectly valid reason to relinquish a bird. Or is it because the bird refuses to go into its cage at night unless country music is playing? If you can't take Garth Brooks every evening, perhaps you should keep looking. It's very hard to turn a country-and-western bird into a Chopin devotee.

Birds are most frequently given up because they are too noisy or because they are aggressive biters. Such was the case with a troubled white cockatoo named Spooky. Spooky had lived with his original family successfully for six years, never causing any problems other than occasionally raising his voice and using the beak on his flashy orange-crested head to bang on his perch. One night, however, Spooky lived up to his name.

While sitting on the sofa with Serena and enjoying a good head-rub, Spooky without warning freaked out and grabbed Serena's lip and bit down hard. Startled, Serena instinctively pulled back, but Spooky hung on for a good ten seconds before deciding to let go. Afterward Serena's lip required several stitches and plastic surgery, and even then her mouth never looked quite the same again. Although Serena adored the well-intentioned Spooky, given what had happened she could never completely trust the bird again.

Not long after the lip-lock fiasco Serena and her husband arrived at my store with Spooky and asked if I could find him a new home. Touched by their desperation, I agreed to keep Spooky and hoped another owner might take pity on him despite his delinquent past, which I clearly explained on a card attached to the cage.

Eventually a pretty young teacher came into the store and seemed rather smitten with Spooky's good looks. Then, after reading the card detailing his "incident," she canvassed the store looking for alternatives but somehow kept returning to Spooky's cage. Finally, after an hour of getting acquainted, she agreed to give him a try.

Before Spooky left the store with the teacher, I suggested possible circumstances that might spark a repeat of Spooky's dangerous behavior and offered preventive measures. For instance, Spooky is no longer offered kisses that might put human lips and nose within beak range. In addition, his cage now sits low on the floor to prevent him from taking swipes at unaware guests' cheeks. I advised the new owner to make certain the bird got at least twelve to fourteen hours of darkness each day. (Darkness keeps a bird's sex drive from becoming overstimulated, which can lead to agitation—much as it does with humans. But we'll get to that subject in Chapter 5).

Finally I proposed that Spooky's new owner take care to note any colors of lipstick or clothing that seem to agitate the bird. As a result, she no longer handles Spooky while wearing her fuchsia cashmere sweater. Bright colors, particularly those with reddish hues, can provoke strange reactions from birds who are stimulated by the brilliant shade. My own kakariki, Katie, nearly gave me a heart attack one night when she hit the red redial button on the speakerphone downstairs while I was upstairs in my bedroom folding laundry. Suddenly I heard the living room fill with a man's voice: "Hello, hello? Who's there?"

Imagine my relief when I peered down from the staircase landing and saw Katie sitting smugly beside the phone while the voice of my former neighbor in Connecticut, whom I'd just telephoned, boomed from the speaker.

~~~~~~

Ultimately, no matter how carefully you select your new bird, unexpected troubles and crises may arise. As with people, birds' personalities evolve as they grow older and as their environment changes. They can become more curmudgeonly or more gregarious. They can stop talking and start biting. They can become unexpectedly promiscuous at middle age.

The good news is that you can manage Polly's behavior in most situations by understanding what makes her tick and what ticks her off and by addressing the problem promptly. The upcoming chapters of *Birds on the Couch* will teach you how to do just that.

Believe me, a little enlightenment and effort might save you from spending $100 an hour on therapy for yourself.

CHAPTER 2

Birds Who Love Too Much:

And other aviary emotions

There is no such thing as normal or not normal.

—DR. RUTH WESTHEIMER

WHO WEARS THE PANTS IN YOUR HOUSE-hold? I'd say it's Polly.

I remember well one woman who owned a majestic green Panama Amazon parrot named Regan for twenty years before she married. The bird took quite a liking to his owner's new spouse, but the couple separated after only five years. The wife and Regan stayed together in the house while the husband moved into a no-pets apartment. Unfortunately, even though the relationship had soured between the human family members, Regan missed having a man around. For weeks after the husband left, the chunky, short-tailed bird moped, unwilling to leave her cage except for an occasional bath in the sink.

Bird possession is often a sticky issue in separation agreements. (If you must share the creature, I recommend the bird visit each parent every other week.) But after witnessing the bird's mood swing, this couple arrived at an amicable arrangement. The woman would call her ex-husband and let Regan listen via speakerphone while they discussed settlement issues. This plan worked well early on, but eventually Regan began to monopolize the phone conversations. As the couple tried to finalize divorce details, the bird would jabber incessantly. Finally, in the middle of a conversation one day, the wife decided that Regan was being just too bothersome. She hung up the speakerphone and picked up a regular phone, essentially cutting the bird off in mid-conversation.

The parrot, however, with her sensitive hearing, could still hear the man's voice emanating from the telephone receiver. Peeved, Regan charged at her owner, trying to grab the phone with her beak. In doing so, she rammed against the woman's face, making a long, painful scratch.

Jealousy? Perhaps. Birds can grow quite attached to people and environments. Take away someone or something they love, and emotional outbursts are to be expected. How you react will either encourage the behavior or put an end to it.

In this particular case, the couple inflamed Regan's jealousy by permitting her to stay in contact with the ex-husband and then abruptly ending that contact. When the conversation was suddenly cut off, who can blame the bird for growing vexed? By flying at the woman's face, Regan was attempting to show her displeasure and also her dominance.

Here's why: Birds by nature are sensitive to pecking orders. Even though you are not a bird, your Polly thinks of you as a member of her flock. Therefore she will instinctively try to control you in subtle and not so subtle ways. She wants you to yelp or open her cage or pay attention to her. When she screams, bites, or flies at you, she is trying to control the

relationship by eliciting a particular reaction from you. In such situations it will be helpful to examine what has changed about Polly's surroundings. What might have made her feel uncomfortable or out of sorts? Forget about yourself for a moment and ask yourself, "How does Polly feel?"

WHAT'S LOVE GOT TO DO WITH IT?

Frequently I'm asked if birds can actually feel human emotions. As narcissistic human beings, it is quite tempting to explain Polly's behavior in terms we understand: "She loves me so much. That's why she always flies to my shoulder and fluffs up when I rub the back of her neck."

Polly may be quite fond of you, but trust me, true love isn't her primary motivation. Pet birds, after all, are still animals and react with the same basic survival instincts as their counterparts in the wilderness. Birds do act in ways that mimic human love, jealousy, fear, and hate. But while there are perfectly logical reasons for much of Polly's behavior, these reasons are different from the ones that motivate humans.

Let's examine why Polly chooses to snuggle with you rather than someone else and why she perches on your shoulder instead of your forearm.

Taller is better to birds. Your importance to a bird increases proportionately to your height. Think about what happens when you approach a group of wild birds outside. They scatter to higher points, right? Birds do this in search of safety. In a bird's mind, moving up is natural because whatever is threatening on the ground can't reach them when they're up high.

Now, why does Polly sit on your shoulder, you may wonder, rather than your outstretched arm? Think again about the same group of wild birds. Few species will sit near the top of a tree where they are exposed. Most will alight on a branch and then move close to the tree's center. The reason: the limbs are more stable there. A gust of wind could cause flimsy branches to sway, which in turn could make a bird lose its balance. The same instinct applies to the human body. Birds perceive your shoulders and head as the less mobile "trunk" of the body, whereas your arms flail about much more. Similarly, birds are often skittish about snuggling up to small children, who tend to dart about more vigorously and seem unstable to birds. Like smaller bushes, children are less secure landing spots, and their fingers aren't perceived as strong branches.

Birds are also attracted to people who readily serve their needs. Many birds, especially the gentle-faced soft gray cockatiels, have an endearing habit of ducking their orange cheeks to be rubbed. When you oblige, they can become quite tranquilized. In fact, you sometimes can calm an agitated bird with proper caressing. This warm response isn't always a testament to your magic touch, however. In truth, Polly might just have an itch.

Twice a year birds lose many old feathers, which are then replaced with fresh new-grown feathers. This new plumage—called pinfeathers—looks like tiny soda straws and can be ticklish to a bird as it grows in. I suspect the sensation must feel somewhat like having itchy curlers in your hair. These pinfeathers have stiff casings around them, which birds pull off with their beaks. But because they can't easily reach the backs of their necks and head, pet birds need you to serve as their masseur.

The best bird strokers are the ones who let their fingers do the walking along Polly's neck, loosening the casings as they go. Do this well, and you'll have Polly completely under your spell.

TALKIN' ABOUT MY BIRD

We hear about birds bonding for life and loyally attaching themselves to their first owner. Whether or not that's true love, I can't say. But I know that I've personally experienced profound relationships with several feathered friends myself. My first parakeet, Skippy, whom I bought when I was ten, could identify my footsteps in our apartment hallway and would always fly to meet me at the front door. Perhaps I'm flattering myself, but I like to think I was someone special to Skippy. After all, he never came to greet Mother.

I also remember a lovely young woman named Amanda who purchased a yellow-collared macaw and named him Bartholomew. I had raised Bartholomew since he was a chick. He would greet me every morning with a hearty hello and flatter me with solicitations of "Hey, pretty girl!" Okay, I'll admit I was sad to see Bartholomew go.

Amanda fell in love with Bartholomew's clear voice and rushed him home, where she expected his verbalizing to continue. No such luck. The bird refused to say a word, despite constant coaxing by a befuddled Amanda. After a few months she telephoned me in desperation, and I agreed to drop by after work to check on Bartholomew. The moment I walked through the door, he immediately resumed his Don Juan act, spewing flattery in my direction. I stayed for a bit and drank a cup of coffee; I'd forgotten how much I liked spending time with Bartholomew.

What likely happened here was that the visual stimulation of seeing me—a memory from his old flock—made him feel less threatened. This familiarity was enough to loosen up his vocal cords, and he continued his boisterous banter even after I left.

Sometimes a bird you thought was faithful will turn fickle in a heartbeat. I recall Chopper, a lovely yellow-naped Amazon parrot who belonged to my close friend Cliff. He had lugged Chopper back from his Peace Corps assignment in Colombia and cared for him with great devotion for nearly a decade. The bird and I maintained a fantastic relationship, chatting like old friends each time I visited. So when Cliff sought me out one afternoon and announced that he was moving away and couldn't take Chopper with him, I had no qualms assuming Chopper's care.

But the strangest thing happened. As I signed the check to buy Chopper from Cliff, the bird looked at us both and obviously thought, *This is absolutely unacceptable.* After Cliff left, Chopper became impossible to handle. He refused to talk, and he lunged at me as I walked by. In Chopper's mind, I was the reason he had lost his true love, and therefore I was the cause of his melancholy state. It didn't matter in the least to Chopper that he had loved me, too, in the past. He couldn't see past the immediate pain of Cliff's departure.

One day my friend Robyn dropped by to visit. Chopper stared at her intently for a moment, fluffed up his green feathers, and seemed enchanted with her. Despite my warnings about his behavior, Robyn bought Chopper soon after. Upon taking him home, she found that Chopper was a perfect gentleman, giving her no trouble whatsoever. I figured Chopper had forgiven me and forgotten Cliff. How naive I was!

One day I stopped by Robyn's house when Chopper happened to be out of his cage. He took one look at my face and, in true Amazon parrot spirit, flew at me in a rage: *There's no way I'm going back to that pet store, lady. I remember you, you're the one who signed the check and drove Cliff away!*

I had never inflicted any harm on Chopper, but he remembered my role in Cliff's disappearance. He never forgave that action, and he convinced me that birds can hold a grudge. Now when I visit Robyn, Chopper is confined to his cage with a blanket hiding me from his view. Personally, though, I've forgiven Chopper. Birds, I know, are flighty creatures.

FASHION-CONSCIOUS POLLYS

Chopper's motivations were clear. But birds can go berserk for much more obscure reasons. Take your nail polish, for instance. Birds have exquisite color vision, and the wrong hue can send them into a persnickety fit. Try reaching into your bird's cage with five bloodred fingernails. Most birds likely will either peck at the polish or back away in alarm—unless you wear this color so consistently that the bird considers it a normal part of your fingers.

Color sensitivity among birds often relates to their own shades. A green bird is rarely threatened by other green objects, but if his wings and tail are bright red and yellow, the bird will notice any red and yellow accessories that you wear.

Any change in your personal appearance can throw Polly for a loop. Little children are sometimes startled when a parent appears with a new haircut. Parents represent stability, and children may be unnerved by any unexpected dramatic change. Birds are the same way. If you change your eyeglass frames, for example, your bird may not immediately recognize you. If your lovebird is accustomed to fluttering about in your long locks, your new short haircut may come as a real shock. By shaving his mustache, a man can elicit the same reaction—concern and perhaps a little cage-rattling and wing-beating.

I don't mean to imply that you should never change your appearance. Just realize that these details could be the reason why Polly is acting a bit out of sorts.

Sometimes a change in your appearance can actually improve communication between you and your bird. One dark-haired woman had a yellow-headed Amazon parrot who rarely gave her the time of day. But one afternoon, perhaps to spite impending middle age, the woman abruptly changed her hair color to blond. Well, the parrot went ape. He couldn't take his eyes off her hair and was prancing about in his cage trying to attract her.

Likewise, my sulfur-crested cockatoo, Bill, was very sensitive to my appearance. Bill was white with a handsome yellow crest. Most cockatoos express themselves by raising or lowering their crest to signal their likes and dislikes. My own hair is—or was, years ago—dark brown. I came down to start the coffee one morning with a yellow towel wrapped around my wet hair. Bill took one look at my new headwear and actually fell off his perch in amazement. Bill thought I was communicating with him by wearing that towel wobbling about atop my head like a crest. I have no idea what he thought I was saying, but I wish I did because he was obviously impressed.

Another sucker for appearance was Charlie, the elderly Amazon parrot who had been handed over to the Animal

Exchange because he was too talkative for his owners to tolerate. Charlie, a typical green parrot with a yellow head, loved anyone with blond curly hair. As soon as he spotted a blond customer entering the store, he would shout, "Hello, how are you?" Customers found this charming and would spend a few minutes doting on Charlie, who subsequently became very full of himself.

"Take me home. I'm so pretty. I'm yours!" he would say none too subtly.

Once when a customer showed up wearing a sweatshirt with a yellow hood, we couldn't resist playing a trick on the conceited Charlie. We asked the dark-haired customer to stand by Charlie's cage with her hood off at first. The bird viewed the customer with mild curiosity until she slowly pulled the hood over her head. The bird's reaction was astonishing. He began to spread his wings and carry on with more enthusiasm than we thought he had left in him. Then she took the hood down, leaving Charlie very confused. It was nice to see the bird humbled and quiet—for once.

The moral here: if Polly's attitude toward you suddenly changes, first try to determine what about you has changed and perhaps distracted her. Then you can either wait and see if she adjusts or go back to your original look. Remember, relationships are all about give-and-take.

WHY THE CAGED BIRD BALKS

If a stranger comes to your door and forces his way inside, your immediate reaction is one of fear and distrust. The same is true of birds. A bird's cage is his refuge, and he prefers his cage to just about anyplace else in the world.

Early on in your relationship, be careful how you approach the cage. If your bird feels that you are invading his territory, he will back up and act defensive toward the intrusive hand reaching inside. However, if at first you move slowly and let him grow accustomed to you standing near the cage and speaking calmly, his reaction will be different. Birds hear very well, and if they are used to hearing your comforting voice reassuring them, they will not be afraid when you approach them.

Remember also that the way to Polly's heart is often through her stomach: feeding her immediately after you open her cage door will lend a friendly tone to the atmosphere.

Think about dogs for a moment. It's typically wise to let a strange dog sniff your hand first before you pet him. That brief moment of nuzzling puts the animal at ease and lets him determine by your scent if you are safe. Polly needs to sense that you are part of her environment—her cage—before she decides that you are safe. That's her way of owning you. Once you become an extension of the cage in her mind, she will feel more comfortable marching up your arm to your shoulder. Stand near the cage when you open the door to let her out. That way she will perceive you as part of her home base, so to speak.

If she is reluctant to venture outside her home, set her cage on the floor and take off its top. Remember, anything higher is better in her mind. The same logic applies to an ornery bird sitting on your shoulder who balks at returning to her cage. Bend down lower than the cage, and suddenly the cage becomes infinitely more appealing because it is now the highest point in sight.

In one of my parrot psychology classes, a lady described an interesting dilemma that sometimes develops when birds live in pairs. She and her husband owned two lovebirds, Molly and Samantha, who lived together harmoniously inside their cage. Whenever they were released, however, the birds became quite aggressive toward each other.

As it turned out, the woman always took Molly from the cage while her husband played with Samantha. The birds in turn became possessive of their respective handlers and exhibited jealous behavior when their owners were involved. In birdspeak, the creatures viewed the humans as an extension of their safe cage. Molly loved the wife and didn't feel secure around the husband because he was unfamiliar. The same was true of Samantha, who was disdainful of the wife. I advised the couple to begin swapping birds—a simple strategy that worked splendidly. Soon Samantha and Molly perceived the couple as a collective part of their cage and ultimately accepted both owners simultaneously into their flock as a complete family.

FROZEN WITH FEAR

One afternoon the telephone rang while I was sweeping up at the store. I picked up the handset and heard a distraught voice on the other end of the line.

"I took my parakeet outside to give him some fresh air, and suddenly a hawk screamed and flew overhead, and now my bird is just sitting in his cage frozen," she said shrilly. "I mean he's standing there with one foot in the air clutching some food, and he won't move. Is he dead?"

I kept sweeping. "No," I told her. "He's not dead. He's just scared. He'll probably be all right in a few minutes. Just take him inside and speak to him in soothing tones." She called back twenty minutes later, audibly more relaxed, and reported that the parakeet seemed perfectly normal.

It was probably the hawk's looming shadow that frightened the bird rather than its loud cry. Birds grow frightened when they see anything moving over them—even a speck of dust. At the store, we insist that children leave their balloons at the front door because the helium-filled orbs would send our birds into a frenzy. This fear is another reason I discourage customers from setting any objects on top of cages. Remember, a bird's instinct when frightened is always to fly, and the presence of something foreign overhead blocks the flight zone. Speaking to anxious birds in a calm, repetitive voice is the best way to smooth any ruffled feathers.

Owners sometimes mistake fear for anger in birds. Angry behavior in people is quite different from what appears to be rage in birds—although perhaps the reasons for bird "anger" should lead us to examine our own anger more carefully.

Andy, the hyacinth macaw who lives in my office, will occasionally yell with a nearly deafening voice. He always does this when the cleaning staff comes to wash and polish the floors. Andy sounds angry, but in reality he's frightened. For some reason, the sound and sight of the floor cleaners absolutely terrifies him. I've tried closing the office blinds and shutting the door, but he always manages to hear the sound and respond to it. I recognize his fear for what it is, and I don't discipline him. Instead, I stay with him and speak to him gently until the cleaners leave.

Ultimately, you are responsible for your bird's emotional well-being, so tread carefully. Birds can be irrevocably scarred by traumatic events, and afterward not much can be done to help them. Ever notice how a dog who has been beaten will always cower at the sight of a raised hand? Or how a child with abusive parents may shy away from physical displays of affection? The emotional makeup of most creatures—humans and animals included—is heavily influenced by significant events, particularly those that occur early in life.

When you bring a new bird into your home, you can never be certain how much love and attention it will require. Polly could have a stiff independent streak or she could prove to be an incredibly high-maintenance pet. My best advice is to stay flexible and open-minded; you'd be surprised how far a little patience and sensitivity will go when dealing with an emotionally erratic bird.

CHAPTER 3

The Bird Who Cried Wolf:

Remember, you wanted him to talk

The cuckoo shouts all day at nothing.

—A. E. HOUSMAN

A MAGICIAN WAS WORKING ON a cruise ship in the Caribbean. The audience was different each week, so the magician allowed himself to do the same tricks over and over again. There was only one problem: the captain's parrot saw the shows each week and began to understand how the magician performed every trick.

Soon the parrot started shouting in the middle of the show: "Look! It's not the same hat!" and "Look! The flowers are under the table" and "Hey, all the cards are the ace of spades."

The audience, amused by the parrot's banter, roared with laughter. The magician was furious but couldn't do anything; after all, it was the captain's parrot.

One day the ship had an accident and sank. The magician found himself adrift on a piece of wreckage in the middle of the ocean with the parrot—of course. They stared at each other with hatred but did not utter a word. The silence went on for a day and another and another.

After a week the parrot finally spoke: "Okay, I give up. Where's the boat?"

So you think you want a bird that talks?

Nearly 99 percent of my customers are determined to buy a bird that can communicate with human words. We are fascinated by the idea of conversing with an animal—especially one that doesn't move its lips. Do birds understand what they are saying and have the ability to reason, as the magician's parrot seemed to do in the joke above? It often seems that way. When my hyacinth macaw, Andy, says, "I," and hears me respond, "Love," he will finish my sentence: "You." He also says "Bye-bye" every night when I leave the store.

Banky, a parrot who lives in Los Angeles, gives his bird-sitter, Ginny, a hard time when she tries to put him to bed each night. Banky is allowed to move about freely outside his cage for most of the day. But at bedtime, when Ginny tries to lure him into his cage, he cries out, "I'm not going in. Please, *please,* Banky not going in!" This exchange continues until finally Banky gives in, telling Ginny, "Ha-ha. All right. Night-night. Banky go sleep-sleep."

Most likely, both Andy and Banky are repeating phrases they've overheard or have been taught, and they enjoy the consistent response they receive from those in the room. Birds imitate what they've heard, particularly those phrases that are

spoken with passion or with regularity—like "good-bye" every time you leave a room. After I said "I love you" repeatedly for months, Andy began to enjoy saying those words himself. And when Banky's owners tried to put him back in his cage during the early stages of his life, they probably said things like: "Please, please, Banky" and "Go in. Go sleep-sleep." The first time Banky repeated the words, he probably received such a splendid shocked reaction from his owners that he continued to repeat himself.

I once boarded an African gray parrot named Delphia at my house. At the time, a rather malleable Irish setter named Jody lived with me as well. The first time Delphia visited, all was peaceful. But when she returned for a second visit she began calling Jody's name in my voice. When Jody came galloping up to the cage, Delphia would try to bite her tail. This continued for a while, with Delphia taking great glee in her ability to torment the naive setter. I worried that if Delphia ever managed to get a chunk of Jody's tail, negative reinforcement would unravel all my efforts to get Jody to come when I called her. So for several days I kept the bird behind closed doors. She of course continued to hail the dog, but Jody couldn't get into the room to respond. Eventually, Delphia grew bored by the lack of response and quit calling Jody altogether. The dog kept her tail, and I kept my sanity.

Although there are no set guidelines, through the years I have found that some birds are naturally more loquacious than others. African gray parrots and yellow-naped Amazons have proved to be particularly gifted conversationalists. Cockatoos, conures, parakeets, and lories have tiny but clear voices, while lovebirds and cockatiels speak with less consistency.

The record for birdspeak proficiency, according to a spokeswoman for the 1998 *Guinness Book of World Records,* is held by a female gray parrot named Prudle who boasted an 800-word vocabulary and won the "best talking parrotlike bird" title at the National Cage and Aviary Bird Show in London every year from 1965 to 1976. Prudle resided in Seaford, England.

Prudle is, of course, an anomaly. So don't demand similar results from your parrot. Such lofty expectations might give Polly an inferiority complex, and insecure birds aren't what we're aiming for in *Birds on the Couch.*

SAILOR-TALKIN' BIRDS

One difficulty with birds who talk is that you cannot teach them to distinguish between what's appropriate speech and what isn't. They just don't care, and for all their intelligence, they have no gift for tact or etiquette—they go for the response instead.

I once boarded a yellow-naped Amazon parrot named Bollo, who had been purchased by a couple of sailors in South America when their cargo ship entered port. On the trip home, Bollo lived on board with the crew and learned language he wouldn't have heard in most reputable pet stores. When the ship returned to the United States, the bird was sold to us at Animal Exchange.

Bollo fit into the Animal Exchange environment very well at first. He was your classic big green parrot with a short tail, and he attracted customers' attention without fail. I figured that finding Bollo a new owner would be a cinch.

One afternoon a tall, elegant elderly woman dressed in a sharp suit and a pillbox hat came into the store and took a look around. Mike, the store manager, was working next to Bollo's cage.

The lady walked past them but didn't see the parrot. Bollo, however, did see her. He stared delightedly at the woman and wobbled happily back and forth on his feet. As she walked by his cage, still not seeing him, he hollered, "That's a nice piece of ass, Mama!"

When she turned to see who was speaking, the only person in sight was Mike, who reddened and quickly hurried into the back of the store to find me. After he told me what had occurred, I immediately went looking for the woman and found her making a beeline for the exit. I explained that the bird had made the offensive remark, but I don't think she believed me.

As I watched her scurry out the door, Chanel purse bumping behind her, I prayed the insolent parrot would hold his tongue. Gratefully, he did. Finding Bollo a new home proved to be more challenging than I had thought.

The message here is to be very, *very* careful what you say around your birds. They are always listening. We were given a parrot who had grown up with a couple whose son had become a juvenile delinquent. Unfortunately the young man didn't listen to his parents' early warnings and died in a gun-shooting incident. The parrot, who obviously *had* listened, would shout, "Do you wanna go to jail? Do you wanna go to jail?" After their son's death, the family could no longer endure the bird's talking and turned him over to Animal Exchange.

Birds pick up things you utter with emotion, which is why they particularly enjoy blasphemies. Try repeating "Hello, hello" in a flat voice; you could say it a thousand times before Polly picks it up. But if you call your husband a lazy good-for-nothin' just once in an outraged voice, don't be surprised when Polly repeats that for guests at your next dinner party.

One of my customers held a soiree during which her African gray parrot committed a rather outrageous faux pas. The party was well under way, with the bird enjoying himself immensely and repeating all sorts of amusing comments from his extensive repertoire. The guests reacted favorably, which excited the bird and encouraged him to continue his performance. Because birds can imitate human voices with frightening accuracy, everyone at the party recognized the hostess's voice when the parrot clearly yelled, "John, are you drinking again?"

It's best to avoid discussing personal problems when your parrot is present. And remember that while repetition is important, birds can pick up phrases uttered only once if the speaker says them with conviction.

Watch what you say.

Before we look at safe ways to build your bird's vocabulary, let's examine a few of the more disconcerting ramifications of owning a talking bird.

First of all, there is no telling when a bird will sound off. She may call out "Damn bird, damn bird" while you talk on the telephone to your son's teacher. Or she might shriek "I'm a *pretty* bird" as you are sneaking her onto an airplane.

These outbursts are inconvenient, to say the least. But they aren't nearly as troublesome as the ordeal my friend Marcia went through with Prince, her gossipy sun conure. Marcia dated a guy named Dan for nearly four years. Dan still lived with his parents, so the couple spent an inordinate amount of time at Marcia's house. Prince accepted this arrangement and even learned to greet Dan graciously by name.

Unfortunately, when Marcia broke up with Dan and started dating again, Prince didn't feel like learning anyone else's name. So he greeted all men indiscriminately with: "Hi, Dan!" It was certainly an icebreaker for first dates, but it took years of hurried explanations on Marcia's part before Prince finally got over Dan and stopped calling his name.

Likewise, a sociable young woman named Tula, who lived on Long Island, came to rue the day she'd taught her parakeet to talk. Several times when Tula brought a young man home for a visit, her bird would announce cheerfully, "Out all night again, huh? Out all night again!"

As the stories of both these young ladies show, a bird's memory can be uncomfortably long. My friends Arnie and Joan own a very vocal spectacled Amazon parrot named Alix. This particular bird is red, white, and blue with a bright yellow beak and little rings of bare skin circling his eyes.

Arnie and Joan live with the bird on a suburban street in Montgomery County, Maryland. Although Alix is a small parrot, he has a penetrating voice and speaks very clearly. The sedate neighborhood is one of freshly cut lawns, elegant houses, and a very strong Neighborhood Watch program. Alix previously belonged to a breeder who, as a joke, taught the bird to say "Help! Help! Let me out!" Whenever the breeder hand-fed Alix, the bird was so eager to get out of the cage and reach the food that the breeder thought this particular phrase was appropriate. Alix never forgot the routine, even after he went to live with Arnie and Joan.

One afternoon, perhaps feeling a bit hungry, Alix experienced birdy déjà vu. He began screaming "Help! Help! Let me out!" to a passerby taking an afternoon stroll. It was summer, and the windows were open, so Alix's voice carried freely into the open streets.

Alarmed, the neighbor called the police, who showed up only to find that the so-called victim was a parrot. Alix was delighted, of course, to see the flashing police car lights and the commotion he caused. His owners have since moved him away from the window, but he remembers the brouhaha that resulted from his previous outburst and continues to yell occasionally, "Help! Help!" The immediate neighbors, who can still hear him, are savvy enough to ignore his screeching, but occasional visitors to the neighborhood have called the police from cellular or pay phones. Fortunately, the authorities now know Alix's proclivity for crying wolf and keep a notation in their records not to respond to emergency calls at Arnie and Joan's home for someone in distress. It's only the bird . . . they hope.

HERE, KITTY-KITTY-KITTY

If you want Polly to talk, there are ways to encourage her to speak—and even to censor her comments. I highly recommend the commercial tapes that repeat particular phrases owners generally like their birds to say. Here's a sample:

I'm soooo pretty.
You are soooo pretty.
Good night. Sweet dreams.
Here's looking at you, kid.
Come closer, my friend.
How about a kiss?
Here, kitty-kitty . . . Meow!

Polly can easily learn these comments and others, particularly if she's exposed to them at an early age. Many tapes also come in different languages for those who want a bilingual bird. One maître d' at a French restaurant had a lovely Panama Amazon parrot with a yellow forehead who, like most Amazons, was fond of showering with his owner. The maître d' frequently sang in the shower, and after several weeks the bird was crooning tunes in French. The bird may not have understood what she was saying, but she definitely recognized how impressed people were with her bilingual abilities. That was enough to keep her going.

Birds can also carry on conversations with each other or with themselves in different voices—which can be as startling as having someone with a multiple personality, like Sybil, in the house. My cockatoo, Bell, sounds just like me when she screams, so I threaten my daughters by telling them that I'm going to will her to them when I die.

You'll do best to train Polly by speaking to her in a high-pitched voice; for some reason birds respond better to sopranos. My voice, which is low and throaty, is largely ineffective for this task. A young child's, however, is perfect. And if you live near a police station or firehouse, don't be startled if an alarm goes off in the middle of your living room. It's probably just Polly, who has become enchanted with the sound of the shrill sirens.

Some birds take well to music performed by high-pitched singers who belt out the same refrain again and again. Billy, a pet parrot, learned to sing a tune called "Mama" from that bubbly British pop group the Spice Girls, according to *Newsweek* magazine. The blue-fronted Amazon reportedly listened to the song over and over again because his owner's daughter was quite taken with the singers and played nothing else on her stereo. Billy's cage-mate, however, was obviously not a Spice Girls fan and boasted a limited vocabulary: "Shut up!" Perhaps he didn't properly understand Girl Power.

In general, television shows aren't a particularly good mechanism for improving a bird's speech. The dialogue, if it's good, typically isn't repeated often enough to interest a bird. Commercials with catchy jingles, however, can work. Remember the cat food commercial where the kitty repeats in a singsongy voice: "Meow, meow, meow, meow . . . Meow meow meow meow"? I knew one bird who drove a cat bonkers by repeating that phrase over and over until finally the cat leaped from a shelf to the bird's cage and knocked it down from the ceiling. If the owner hadn't been home to rescue the bird, that could have been a terminal experience. It just goes to show that watching too much TV really can be unhealthy.

As fast as birds can learn to speak, they can also quickly forget everything you've slaved to teach them. Depending on your bird's particular talents, this can be a stroke of luck or a terrible disappointment. One nice family, the Dunns, decided to purchase a female cockatiel as a companion for their male. Now, the male was a suave fellow who had learned a vast repertoire of tunes from Mr. Dunn, including a love song called "Eternally." Obviously, any hen in her right mind would have fallen for him. Sure enough, he charmed his new partner right away. However, no sooner had they bonded than he abruptly stopped singing. (Perhaps once he secured a mate he no longer felt the need to woo his woman; my friends often complain about this phenomenon with the men they date.)

The Dunns were dismayed and separated the two birds because they missed hearing "Eternally," but the male continued to verbalize only in parrotspeak. Eventually the family gave up and let them move back in together where they chirped birdie talk to their hearts' content, but no strains of "Eternally" ever floated from behind those bars again. The moral is that a bird who has learned humanspeak can suddenly change his tune when a member of his own species is introduced. Think of the challenge of learning a foreign language: if everyone's speaking it, you're more apt to follow suit. But as soon as someone speaking your native language enters the group, it's altogether too easy to revert to what you know best. I recommend sticking with one bird if you want a smart-talking Polly.

SAY IT AIN'T SO

There are certain times when you can count on Polly to chatter. Birds routinely vocalize in the morning and evening. When the sun goes down, the volume is sometimes so deafening here at Animal Exchange that I've considered buying earplugs for some of my more sensitive employees and customers.

Birds also talk when they are lonely. When your bird can't see you, she wants your attention. So she screams. And what do you instinctively do? You come running—which is exactly what the bird had in mind. So how does Polly think she'll get you back? She'll keep on yelling. I suggest letting her scream all she wants the first few times but don't respond, no matter how loud she yells.

The one time birds are sure to pipe down is while they are nesting. This behavior can be traced back to their basic instincts: why announce to a prowling predator that you and your babies are available for dinner? Smart birds stay hush-hush when they are nesting. Typically they spend about three weeks to a month laying and hatching their eggs, so you are guaranteed a quiet reprieve at least once or twice a year, depending on your bird's breeding schedule.

Although controlling Polly's yammering once she starts isn't easy, there are some subtle techniques that can prove handy. One simple tactic is to adjust the bird's feeding schedule. For instance, the owner of a pair of mitered conure parrots once told me his birds were loud in the morning and again in the evening. But, he explained, they seemed to settle down after he fed them. I suggested feeding them earlier.

At the last party you went to I'll bet everyone chattered during cocktail hour and then settled down during dinner. First of all, filling your mouth prevents you from talking unless you are rude. It's the same with birds. They will concentrate on nibbling rather than vocalizing if given the choice. Most of us are less outgoing and active after a big meal; it's harder to raise hell on a full stomach.

Toys are also a good way to keep a bird occupied. A bird has less reason to vocalize if he's busy chewing apart his Polly Dolly—a very entertaining contraption made of cloth, twine, and leather. Long twigs with bells dangling from one end are also a great distraction. But I advise you to change your bird's toys from time to time and to move them around in the bird's cage now and then. Toys are like meals: meat loaf and potatoes every day of the week will soon become boring.

Ultimately, however, birds will decide when, if, and where they will talk. So it pays to make certain that you and the people around you can live with this unpredictability. When I first opened the store, we hand-fed two cute baby sun conures, which are about three times the size of parakeets when fully grown. Both of them came back to us several times from different owners who couldn't tolerate their loud voices. We try to make sure a buyer's lifestyle is compatible with a bird's personality traits, but sometimes we misjudge both person and creature.

One of these baby sun conures seemed like a good match with a young man named Pete, a bartender who lived alone in an apartment and desired companionship. Soon these two were eating, watching television, and bathing together. During the day while his neighbors were working, Pete—who didn't have a girlfriend—taught the bird phrases he obviously wanted to hear from a lover. This soon proved problematic.

Pete's job at the bar kept him out late, and at first the sun conure waited up quietly each night, listening for her owner's footsteps. Soon, though, the bird grew so attached to the man that she began to pine for his return from work.

One night, as Pete wearily climbed the three flights of stairs to his apartment at 3:00 A.M., the bird began screaming and yelling phrases Pete had taught her: "Hello, hello! Pete's my man. He can do it, yes he can! My, my, look at Pete!"

Unfortunately, Pete's neighbors weren't charmed by the bird's devotion and rhyming skills. During several weeks of similar incidents, Pete became increasingly embarrassed by his bird's affection and his neighbors' complaints. Ultimately, he returned the sun conure to Animal Exchange. I hope he found a human girlfriend to keep him company instead.

Companionship, of course, is what many people seek in a talking bird. After all, society expects certain birds to carry on conversations, and that allows owners to talk aloud to them without feeling silly. My mother is ninety-four years old, and I attribute much of her vivacious nature to her long owner-ship of various birds, which have kept her company since my father died. I remember her once telling me matter-of-factly: "It's nice not to have to talk to chairs, Ruth."

Betty, who is eighty-seven, visits a senior center in Maryland regularly and is a loyal participant in my Lend-a-Pet program. Slender and attractive, she was once a dancer and now devotes her energy to maintaining an enormous garden of flowers and vegetables. Over the years she has adopted three or four birds through the Lend-a-Pet program, welcoming them into her home and feeding them tidbits from her garden. In return, the birds keep Betty company with calls of "Good morning," "Hi there!" and "Whatcha doin'?"

A sweet-natured sun conure named Helmut ultimately proved to be the most loyal friend Betty could have wanted. Helmut kept to himself around other people, not saying much to the visitors who liked to stroll through Betty's fine gardens. He was always polite, sitting patiently on a stranger's finger-tip without biting, but he talked only when he and Betty were alone. Even then his remarks were limited to "Night-night, Betty" and "Helmut loves Betty."

They had been together for nearly thirteen years when Betty began suffering from memory loss. Occasionally she would forget where she had planted the poppies or the tulips. When her grandchildren stopped by on weekends, Betty would sometimes have to be gently reminded of their names.

During a visit to Animal Exchange, Betty confided to me that the worst episode had occurred one evening when she was filling out the forms for a new health insurance plan. Suddenly she couldn't remember her own name. She panicked and tried to call her daughter, but she couldn't recall the phone number.

Betty sat frozen, tears welling up in her eyes, until a tiny voice piped up from the corner: "Helmut loves Betty. Betty loves Helmut."

The bird's voice jogged Betty's memory. With the mention of her name, she remembered her daughter's number and quickly dialed. They talked for several minutes until Betty was calm enough to finish filling out the forms.

No other pet can give that gift, the gift of humanlike communication. So for all the woes sometimes caused by a bird's speech, their speaking ability remains one of their greatest charms, particularly when they are well coached and living with someone who appreciates or, as in Betty's case, needs their aptitude.

CHAPTER 4

Taming That Tyson Bird:

What was it about his childhood that makes him bite?

> *When a member of my family complains that he or she has bitten his tongue, bruised her finger, and so on, instead of the expected sympathy I put the question, "Why did you do that?"*

— SIGMUND FREUD

IT WAS ONE OF THE MOST SHOCKING actions ever seen on television.

On the evening of June 28, 1997, two top boxing champions, Mike Tyson and Evander Holyfield, faced each other in the ring for a much-anticipated heavyweight rematch. But instead of a great sporting event, the fight would be recorded in the annals of sports history as a public debacle.

Mike Tyson claims that midway through the fight, which was being watched by 1.9 million pay-TV viewers, Evander Holyfield illegally began head-butting him. Tyson had learned at an early age that quick retaliation often brought the best results. As he battled Holyfield that night, he was acting on instinct. He panicked and instinctively bit Holyfield's ear in one swift, horrific movement.

Several months later during an interview with a television newsmagazine show, Tyson said, "There's no doubt about it, I totally lost it. . . . Anything from any kind of functional thinking or any kind of rational thinking was totally out the window. . . . I don't know what happened that night."

You might well ask what Mike Tyson—suspended boxing champion, noted juvenile delinquent, and convicted rapist—could possibly have to do with birds. I'm reminded of a bird club meeting I once attended and the mayhem that ensued.

It was late September, and the summer heat was lingering longer than I or my birds would have liked. We were all slightly edgy, as will happen when animals and people spend too much time struggling to keep their bodies—and their tempers—cool. It was in this frame of mind that I arrived at my friend Don's house along with about thirty-five other club members for our monthly bird chat. Crowded in Don's living room along with several of his birds, we exchanged tales of our pets' escapades during the previous weeks. Although the air conditioner was running and lemonade was served, we were nevertheless uncomfortably warm. My shirt was sticking to my back, and Don's birds were antsy and bug-eyed, unhappy with the temperature and all the strangers milling about in the living room. Because they don't sweat, the birds would spread their wings and pant silently, their beaks hanging open in a rather foolish-looking manner.

Don was a retired army officer whose collection of birds filled the house upstairs and down and spilled over into a

small air-conditioned trailer in the driveway. For this particular meeting, he and his wife had brought several of the larger creatures inside the house to show off to the group. Barrel-chested and proud of his military career, Don strutted about hoping we would be appropriately awed by his vast assemblage of birds. While I was making friends with a sweet doe-eyed green parakeet, Don decided to let loose his biggest bird, a hyacinth macaw with deep blue plumage and a yellow eye ring. If I had known about this decision in advance, I would have warned him against it—particularly given the intense atmosphere in that tiny hot room. But I did not, and Don's mine-is-bigger-than-yours display cost him dearly.

Agitated by the crowd and ill-tempered from the heat, the macaw reacted much like Mike Tyson. Sitting on Don's shoulder, the hum of the crowd in her ears, she simply lost it. In one fell swoop, she zoomed in and chomped on Don's ear, puncturing the earlobe and sending the visitors into a tizzy, which only encouraged the bird to further mayhem. To Don's credit, he never screamed, even though his predicament was worse than Evander Holyfield's because there was no referee to halt the bird club meeting. So the proud army man simply swallowed hard, pulled the bird off his head, and returned her to the safety of her secure cage. Several drops of blood trickled from his head. Don discreetly wiped his now pierced ear and, as they say in the service, carried on.

I felt very bad for Don, but I also knew—to borrow Tyson's words—that "there was some serious stuff going on" in that macaw's head. She was frightened. In a sea of unfamiliar faces, she was forced out of the sanctuary of her cage and expected to behave calmly. There was no way that was going to happen.

We've already seen that cages are safe places for birds. They can come to know and trust you, but they may still perceive strangers and new situations as threatening. Therefore when this macaw was taken from her cage and thrust in front of strangers, she reacted in an extreme manner. Looking for extra support, she used Don's ear as her anchor. Don, had he not been so eager to boast about his bird, might have thought better of removing her under such circumstances and permitting her to perch on his shoulder. Scared by the alien faces and commotion, she was determined to stay put and used everything she could to hold on—including her powerful beak.

Controlling any situation is half the battle with biting birds. Remember, birds appreciate responses, and most people aren't as stoic or as tough as Don. When a bird clamps down on bare flesh with its sharp beak, the automatic reaction is typically *"ouch!"* followed by something unprintable—which, as we have learned, the bird may repeat with glee. Yelping only encourages the biting, because birds like a passionate response.

The same is true of some human relationships. Take, for instance, the ex-lover who constantly calls and provokes you to tears or anger. As long as you react, your ex-lover will maintain control because he can elicit a response. If you don't respond, he will lose that power. It's the same with birds and biting. Any response you give to birds—young birds, in particular—will impress them, sometimes permanently. Many birds have taught their owners to say "No!" or "Ow!" in response to a strategically placed peck with their beak. Other owners are prompted to scream profanities, which the bird, of course, can repeat. Who says you train the bird? It's usually the other way around.

THE RUNAROUND BIRD

The Simon family had recently purchased a beautiful little parakeet named Bluebird, who was like a third child to them. Unfortunately, every time they let him out of the cage, Bluebird would chase the two human children around the house. The kids, ages nine and eleven, unwittingly encouraged the game by running from room to room screaming at the top of their lungs, with the hyper parakeet soaring enthusiastically behind. When Bluebird caught up with the children, he would often bite them, eliciting even more exquisite howls. The salty tears that often followed were just a bonus.

The children's yelling was only one reason for Bluebird's lashing out. He also bit Mr. and Mrs. Simon each time they opened the cage to feed him or to replenish his water. While still inside the cage, he would charge at them furiously. If they let him loose, Bluebird would dive-bomb their hands and arms as if to say "Keep away from my house. This is my property." It pleased Bluebird greatly when, with each bite, the big human hand would jerk away, followed by a hardy "Ouch! Damn bird!"

The distraught Simons arrived at my store one cloudy Sunday fully intending to give up Bluebird for good. No one in the family was happy, except the unsuspecting Bluebird. The Simons figured the bird was going to starve to death because they couldn't get any food inside his cage—not to mention the fact that they were going through a box of bandages each week to cover the damage to their fingers.

After about thirty minutes of counseling, however, I persuaded them to give the little parakeet one more chance. As the rain drizzled outside the store, I trimmed Bluebird's primary and secondary feathers on one wing while he watched me curiously. The clipping prevented him from chasing the children around the house. When he tried to fly, he could break his fall, but he could not catch the kids. (I'll explain how you can trim a bird's wings yourself in Chapter 7.)

Next, I suggested the Simons buy a thick pair of leather gloves to wear when they fed Bluebird and cleaned his cage. After thanking me, they dashed for the car to keep Bluebird from getting wet from the rain and headed home. Three weeks later my phone rang in the store. The Simons were ecstatic. Bluebird at first had shifted into typical dive-bomber mode the moment they reached inside his cage. But when his bites evoked no response, he grew disenchanted with the game. He continued his attacks for a while but finally grew bored with biting and settled down on Mrs. Simon's shoulder as she changed his food and cleaned his cage. Patience paid off for the Simons. I usually remind customers that they may have to refuse to respond a hundred times for each time they have yelped.

SHHHHH!

I realize, however, that it's difficult to stay calm when a bird is clamped tightly to your body tissue. Birds don't have teeth, but they do have hard-pointed beaks backed by tremendous force from their strong neck muscles. A cockatiel can draw blood faster than a nurse, while a hyacinth macaw, who can easily open Brazil-nut shells with his beak, can not only pierce your ear but also inflict substantial damage to your finger. I've had parrots mistake my fingers for nutshells and try to peel my nails off. Such misperceptions can result in serious damage. Even a little parakeet can cause considerable pain by holding on to your cuticle with his beak.

To avoid being bitten, you can wear gloves, as the Simons did, or even a scarf or earmuffs to protect your head and ears. I always try to speak calmly to a bird when I'm working in its cage, and I move my hands slowly and calmly, especially with new birds. Also, it's only fair to give a new bird a reasonable chance to settle in before you expose it to wild parties or rambunctious children, both of which can greatly upset an otherwise serene bird. Agitation of any kind can lead to ruffled feathers and, therefore, biting.

I've also learned a few other tricks through the years that will help dissuade a bird from biting. Toys and food are good distractions for biters, just as they are for excessive talkers, because they keep the bird occupied while you complete your task in the cage. Many birds particularly like plastic rings for climbing or a bell to ring or bump with their head. A particular favorite with parakeets is Penguin Kelly, a stand-up toy that never falls down, even when birds bat it around with their beaks.

Giving your bird lots of hard food will keep the beak from growing and becoming too long and sharp. Parrots need to shell nuts and eat a hard pellet diet to keep their beaks properly filed down. Birds' tongues are very dry and strong. No wet kisses for these animals. They use the tongue to crush their food, removing shells with their beaks. Again, all this activity helps keep a beak focused on something besides your hand.

When teaching a bird that biting is a no-no it's important to respect the bird's emotional state.

A baby bird explores the world with its beak, using it as a third hand, for balance and to test things—just as human children use both feet to climb monkey bars but need a hand to keep themselves from falling. Watch as Polly moves about her cage; she will typically lead with her beak as she walks or climbs. She is testing the stability of each rung or bar she touches. She also needs her beak for balance, just as children need their hands.

Therefore, a parrot will reach for your hand with her beak and hold on until she's certain your finger will stay put as she climbs aboard. If you pull back, the bird will hold on tighter, because she feels unsteady. The next time she will hold on tight right away because she remembers your pulling away. The bird may mean no harm, but of course this feels exactly like a bite to the recipient.

The best way to avoid getting hurt if a bird grabs your finger is to push your hand toward her mouth instead of pulling away. This keeps the bird off-balance and prevents her from tugging at your skin. Usually the bird will then let go and step onto your finger. Saying "Step up" as the bird moves will help reinforce the letting-go behavior and give you a verbal command to use as a cue for the bird not to bite. It also reassures you that your hand is safe and there's no need to pull back.

Unfortunately, remembering to push in instead of pulling away is as difficult as remembering to turn in the direction of a skid when you're driving on ice. Your instinct is to do exactly the opposite, so it will take some discipline and probably a few painful wounds before you remember. At least with biting birds, you won't have to call a tow truck if you panic and forget.

LIGHTS, CAMERA . . . OUCH!

Throughout the years, local TV producers have found that the inhabitants of Animal Exchange make for irresistible camera footage. The stations love to broadcast feature stories at the store because birds are natural performers and exhibitionists. Television reporters quickly become enamored with the idea of capturing my birds' antics on film. However, I've learned that most journalists aren't well acquainted with birds' idiosyncrasies or their tendency toward schizophrenic behavior when a large camera is looming.

One year, as spring approached, the local stations were eager to air some lighthearted stories. Because crazy animal antics always interest viewers, one station sent Henry, one of our better local newscasters, to Animal Exchange. Henry was immaculately dressed, self-assured, and poised on camera. He arrived at the store in early March to check out the various creatures and plan a noon segment about my parrot psychology classes. He chose to feature a heavyset yellow-naped Amazon parrot named Pedro in his closing segment. Henry's idea—unbeknownst to me—was to whisk Pedro from his shoulder onto his hand for an up-close-and-personal final shot. Certainly this would have made for good television. But had Henry asked, I would have warned him that Pedro wouldn't willingly make such a transition, especially with a television camera looming nearby. Unfortunately, Henry didn't ask.

When the moment arrived, Henry reached as planned onto his shoulder for Pedro. The parrot, feeling his environment suddenly becoming quite unstable, balked and looked for something to hold on to. He chose Henry's ear. As Henry pushed harder on Pedro's chest, the bird held tighter to Henry's ear. Henry, who firmly believed that the show must go on, continued to push, hoping the bird would cooperate. Pedro never relented, of course, and Henry ended up sinking to the floor on his knees, doubled over in pain, as the cameraman captured the entire episode. The TV crew tried to stifle their laughter, but to no avail. There was nothing I could do until the filming was through and I could rescue Henry from Pedro's clutches. I apologized profusely, but I secretly thought the episode illustrated the segment's theme quite nicely: one of the most useful lessons customers learn in parrot psychology class is to expect the unexpected. (Fortunately for Henry, the segment was edited in time for the noon news.)

There wasn't much Henry could have done to protect himself in that case. Yelling at Polly is always a no-no when she bites, as is smacking her. You should never hit a bird under any circumstances. We often get calls after it is too late to salvage a situation. Such was the case with Mr. Jones who strangled his parrot when he was nuzzling with the bird and the creature bit his nose. (This was after Mr. Jones had spent months training the parrot not to bite his fingers.) When the parrot clamped on to Mr. Jones's nose and forced a loud scream from the startled man, the response encouraged the bird to hold tighter. In dreadful pain, Mr. Jones began to choke the bird until it finally went limp and released its hold.

Mr. Jones should not have let the bird near his face, particularly since he knew about the bird's earlier finger-biting addiction. Be aware of the dangers of playing kissy-kissy and snuggling with your Polly, especially if she is inclined to use her beak on bare skin.

Another visitor to Animal Exchange asked me if I sold bird muzzles, and when I told her absolutely not, she asked me if duct tape would work equally well. "Don't even think about it," I said. Polly can't eat like that, and she won't learn anything from having her beak latched shut—except that her owner is incredibly cruel, and the tape could kill her by blocking the breathing apparatus. Please don't ever try to punish a bird without checking with a pet store or veterinarian about what's acceptable and what's cruel or dangerous. Punishing is really not an option with birds; redirecting their behavior to something acceptable is the only way to go.

One final word about biting. Birds can become overanxious and ornery when they have a sudden surge of hormones in their tiny systems. This typically happens when they are preparing to breed. The effect isn't unlike what happens when a teenager enters puberty, a time when a rush of new feelings can lead to some unpredictable behavior. It's the same with birds. But instead of arguing with parents or staying out past curfew, Polly's best form of expression often is to bite.

During mating, biting is a useful skill. When mounting a hen, a male bird instinctively holds tight to her neck feathers with his beak to balance himself and take control in bed, in a manner of speaking. Imagine what it would be like for a man to try to stand atop a basketball without holding on with his hands somewhere else. Not so easy, right?

The important lesson to be learned here is that during such heady periods, you can accidentally get in the way of a beak. A bird may take a swipe at you because he is riled up or, occasionally, because he mistakes you for a potential mate. And this sort of love . . . well, it *does* hurt. During such incidents, it may seem you've got a very kinky bird on your hands. But truly, Polly is just feeling amorous.

Which leads us to our next chapter . . .

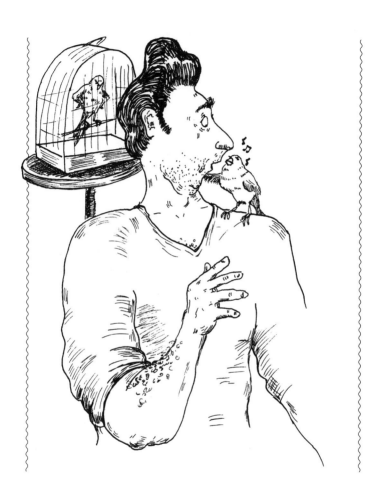

CHAPTER 5

The Woody and Tweetie Complex:

A *Kama Sutra* for birds

Birds do it, bees do it,
Even educated fleas do it.

—COLE PORTER, "LET'S DO IT"

LATE ONE SPRING AFTERNOON A FEW years back I was feeding birds at the store when a large black Cadillac pulled into the parking lot of Animal Exchange. From the driver's side stepped an immaculately dressed woman, probably in her late seventies, who seemed rather agitated. I watched as she hastily removed a brass birdcage from the backseat of the car and then strode inside the store, clutching the cage tightly to her breast.

She looked around impatiently, so I promptly put down my seed pitcher and went to greet her. "May I help you?" I asked.

"I hope so," she replied shrilly. "I think my bird, James Henry, is ill. He's been acting quite strange for several days now."

I pointed out that I was not a veterinarian and could not properly diagnose and treat her bird and offered to recommend some doctors who could. She ignored me and continued anyway. "Please look at him. Maybe you can figure out what's wrong," she pleaded. "I just don't understand his behavior."

So I looked at James Henry. Inside the cage was a sturdy young parakeet climbing happily on his plastic rings. He looked back at me. "What are you staring at?" he seemed to be saying. *"I don't know,"* I thought to myself. *"You look fine to me."* So I asked out loud, "What makes you think James Henry is sick? He looks quite content."

The woman wrung her hands and then lowered her voice. "Well, for starters, he spit up food into my ear this morning. It was really so unpleasant. And then . . ." She held out her arms, exposing two soiled spots on the cuff of her silk shirt. "And *then,*" she repeated, "he keeps making these wet spots on my hands and arms when I stroke him."

There was a stir inside the store as a few eavesdropping staff members turned their backs to keep from laughing. I shot a stern look in their direction but struggled to keep a straight face myself. The woman watched me, waiting for an answer. I smiled reassuringly at her.

"Why, ma'am, I don't believe James Henry is sick at all," I said. "I'm afraid he's just horny."

WHY DO BIRDS FALL IN LOVE?

As James Henry's owner stared at me in horror, I encouraged her to take the bird to the veterinarian if she wished, to make certain he was fine. But as I carefully explained, the parakeet's actions were definitely signs of a healthy, hormonally active bird.

For example, I told her, the wet spots James Henry had left on her silk shirt after rubbing back and forth so sweetly on her arm were secretions of love—just as with humans. What's more, with no other birds around, he seemed to have chosen his owner as a mate.

"Isn't that grand?" I said cheerfully. "He really adores you."

Apparently she didn't think so, judging by the red splotches creeping up her neck. I tried to ease her discomfort by explaining that of course she wouldn't really be expected to act as James Henry's mate in the carnal sense. He would simply use her hands occasionally as a safe spot for masturbating.

For some reason, that didn't console her, either. She picked up the brass cage—this time holding it at arm's length—and mumbled something about checking all this with a doctor. As she walked out of the store, James Henry, bless his heart, jumped to the edge of the cage and chirped charmingly at his owner.

"You hush, you," she hissed at him. "Don't do that."

"He's just saying 'I love you,' " I called after her helpfully.

If she had stayed a bit longer, I could have explained that this was James Henry's time of the year, so to speak. Days are longer in the springtime, and more daylight often increases hormone production, copulation, and egg production among birds. A bird's sex drive in general depends in large part on its living conditions. A well-fed bird with lots of good sunlight and a clean, spacious cage frequently will be more sexually ambitious than one in less prime conditions. Think of how people sometimes like to set the mood for lovemaking. Well, that works with birds too, but instead of cozy candlelight, a big bed, and a fine wine, they are stimulated by broad daylight, a roomy cage, and a good diet of crunchy birdseed and whatever scraps you can spare from your own plate. (No avocado please; it tends to kill parakeets.)

It's helpful to recognize a bird's lustful behavior for exactly what it is so you don't think the animal has just gone berserk or, worse yet, is deathly ill, as James Henry's fastidious owner assumed he was. Come to think of it, I never did find out what happened to James Henry. His owner never returned to the store.

While courtship among parrots includes many different forms of display, another popular but often unsettling means of expression is food regurgitation. Many birds will deposit a nice little wad in their owner's hand, neckline, or ear, as James Henry did with his prim owner. A parakeet who is lucky enough to have a mirror in his cage often will ardently cover the glass with regurgitated food because he thinks he sees a potential mate in the reflection. Narcissism at its finest. Ain't love grand?

Another form of seduction is the prenuptial molt, when birds replace their feathers with more vibrant plumage. This occurs before the breeding season again. During that time, the male in his newly grown finery tries to impress and woo females. This molting process seems to increase his urge to mate as well. Clothes make the man, after all. Just think of the peacock strutting his stuff.

When their hormones are raging, birds of all types will rub themselves vigorously against their perch or favorite toy to relieve pent-up tension. Often they don't care who's in the room, so keep this in mind when you're entertaining, because, yes, they are in fact masturbating.

One little blue male parakeet named Georgia seemed to fall in love with his perch every spring. As he grew older, the cage would vibrate more and more wildly as Georgia pleasured himself. The rattling became so violent that his perplexed owner finally called me and was very relieved when I explained that birds can grow more amorous with age. Perhaps Georgia wasn't too old to have a girlfriend, I suggested. I'm always amused to answer the phone at work and hear the rattle of a cockatiel enjoying himself in his cage in the background. Typically the owner is concerned about this puzzling behavior and has called to see if the bird is okay. "Yes, your bird is okay," I tell them. "In fact he's more than okay—he's *great.*"

However, I hope I'm not too bold in pointing out that it's not always fun to masturbate alone. (I'm still referring to birds, mind you.) They will stand on their perches and call loudly for you to massage the sides of their tails. Most people do that anyway without understanding the sexual ramifications of the stroking. It's absolutely okay and safe: just rub Polly lightly on either side of her rump. But like James Henry, Polly may leave you a little wet present. This only means the rubbing feels *especially* good to her.

GETTING DOWN TO BUSINESS

Before we further explore the intricacies of the birds and the bees—or just the birds, I suppose—perhaps a brief explanation of avian sexual behavior will help.

Birds have one external opening that releases all their urinary, digestive, and sex products. Male birds do not have external penises. Fertilization is accomplished by the male on top of the female, swiping his tail underneath as she raises hers and depositing sperm from his opening into hers. Please observe the sparrows in the street next spring for more graphic details. They can provide a good overview of the process.

Many owners call me in April or May to report that their previously wonderful pet bird has suddenly become a lunatic. Perhaps the bird is sitting grumpily in her cage, attacking anyone who dares to come near her. Or maybe she ruffles her feathers and whines plaintively every time her owner enters the room. Other birds dilate their pupils and lift their tails in the air. This behavior is a means of soliciting attention. One yellow-naped Amazon parrot named Thomas was so docile throughout most of the year that he slept with his owner. But one year Thomas turned nasty after molting and then would attack his bell and try to bite anyone who passed by his cage. He also refused to come to bed with his owner.

Thomas was ready for sex.

Sure enough, he settled down nicely as soon as his owner brought him a lovely little hen.

Sex between birds can be very slam-bam-thank-you-ma'am, or it can be lengthy, tender, and filled with happy pillow talk. Some species are furtive in their efforts, waiting until you've left the room to "do it" in a nest box. Others are quite the little exhibitionists. Take Pretty Boy and Sweetie Pie, two cockatiels who were very vocal when breeding. Just like people, they seemed to want a lot of practice time before they got down to raising a family. These were birds who really should have lived in the promiscuous 1970s. Every morning after a little nap, they would settle into arduous lovemaking, not caring who in the house overheard. It's uncertain whether they were attempting to actually reproduce and failing, or if they were just doing it because "it" felt good. All I know is that not all copulation results in babies.

Birdy passion can vary depending on the birds' size. Larger species take longer to mature—ten years or more, sometimes—while parakeets like James Henry may want to breed enthusiastically before one year of age. Often, however, a lot of practice goes on before chicks are produced.

Birds are fairly monogamous. Even if you put a mating couple in the cage with stranger birds, they typically will copulate only with their "spouse." Occasionally, however, I've known "married" birds who fooled around on the side. If that happens, don't worry. It won't hurt the female one way or another if she has a little quickie with another bird in the same cage. My customers often seem squeamish at this notion of a threesome, but I tell them, "What difference does it make to Polly?" She's not worried about questions of morality. She just wants to lay her eggs.

EGGING POLLY ON

A hen who is preparing to lay eggs can become really charged up. She doesn't need a male to lay eggs, although she does need him to lay eggs that are fertile and will hatch. Believe me, this biological necessity isn't as obvious to the average bird owner as one might assume.

Consider the woman who strode into Animal Exchange brandishing a beautiful teacup. Inside the cup lay an egg, tiny and perfect, produced by her female parakeet who had lived alone for years and spent a lot of time playing in the china closet. The woman looked at me and, with a straight face, asked me to please hatch the unfertilized egg. As patiently as possible, I explained the basics of reproduction to her and confessed that while I considered myself handy with birds, I've never been able to fertilize an egg that is already safely sealed in a shell.

Female birds are able to produce eggs throughout the year. An egg comes out either fertilized or unfertilized. If a male is present to inseminate the female, an egg will be fertilized in her oviduct and sent next to the egg-white gland. Its next stop is the shell gland, where the egg gets its final protective shell coating. I think the process is like the manufacturing of a car as it moves down the assembly line, or like chocolate being produced and packaged at Willy Wonka's candy factory. To me, egg laying is truly one of the most efficient reproductive processes among animals or humans.

This process can be a tremendous drain on a bird's body, however. Females who are about to lay eggs often sit on the floor of their cage and appear cranky and depressed, even though there is no mate around. The egg can also cause uncomfortable backups in other bodily functions. A female parakeet who produces an abnormally large dropping, perhaps the diameter of a penny, is probably about to lay an egg. This, I would assume, cannot feel good.

Of all reproductive behavior, egg laying is perhaps the most startling to new owners. As with puppies and kittens, many people buy baby birds when they are still young and sweet. I always interrupt their fawning to offer a dose of reality. I remind them that this cute baby will grow up into an adult bird, with big-bird attitudes and behavior patterns. As the little pile of feathers matures, she may even produce an egg, which could change her entire personality.

How a female acts during egg production can depend on her relationship with an owner. One of the most amazing avian love stories I ever heard featured Matt and his umbrella cockatoo, Valentine. Matt would sit comfortably in his easy chair cuddling Valentine and stroking her feathers while they watched television. One evening Matt called the store breathless; he had been channel-surfing with Valentine as usual when she suddenly laid an egg in his hand. I tell this tale to students in my parrot psychology classes to show just how strong the bond between owner and bird can grow. Matt was almost as happy as a new father when I explained that Valentine's willingness to share such an experience with him showed how much she trusted him.

Many customers, however, don't want to deal with the egg laying and ask for a boy when bird-shopping. The problem is that, until chicks are produced, it's very difficult to distinguish male birds from females in many species without DNA testing. A few bird types, like cockatiels, begin to look different as they mature depending on their sex. A normal male cockatiel, for instance, will boast a bright yellow face by about eight months of age, while a female will continue to have the gray face of a baby. Both have lovely orange cheeks, unless they are among the new white-faced mutations that have recently surfaced. Another way to determine the sex of cockatiels is to listen for the lovely songs a male will sing as he matures.

Some people think you can tell males and females apart by the way the pelvic bones are spaced—closer together for males, farther apart for females. I can only say that I haven't found this method to be very accurate. Because customers are often intent on a boy bird, unscrupulous sellers will assure them that a bird is a male even if they can't tell the difference. I can't tell you how many calls I've received from baffled customers who didn't understand why John, their parrot, just laid an egg.

Well, that isn't John, I tell them. It's Julie.

TAMING POLLY'S LIBIDO

There are ways to curb your bird's lascivious behavior if it becomes bothersome. For starters, make certain you aren't unconsciously flirting with your pet or unwittingly giving off sexual signals. Birds, as we have learned, respond well to other birds who are similarly colored. They do the same thing with humans. One day I wore a white shirt, and a white cockatiel climbed up my arm and passionately courted my sleeve. Trust me, people stared.

In general, the easiest and most effective way to give Polly the equivalent of a cold shower is simply to decrease the amount of time she is exposed to daylight. In most cases, cutting light back to ten hours a day or less, putting Polly to bed earlier and waking her later, will do wonders to cool raging hormones. You can always throw a thick cover over her cage during the day to make her think it's nighttime. The darkness slows down a bird's natural urge to reproduce by reducing hormone levels. Please remember, however, that birds don't eat in the dark; therefore full-time darkness is not an option.

Often birds will develop a particularly annoying habit of ringing a bell when they are in the mood for love. It's their way of demanding attention or releasing pent-up frustration. There's a simple way to stop this: remove the bell from the cage. You can return it after Polly's hormonal stampede has slowed a bit.

Birds grow new feathers when they molt and prepare for courtship, and this process is very fatiguing. Moreover, they need calcium to allow the new feathers to develop properly and to aid in eggshell formation if they are female. Nutritional deficiencies can produce a very tired, fussy bird, which you don't want. Ground oyster shells and cuttlebones are good for a bird to chew during these periods. These are sold at most pet stores that cater to birds.

If your single pet bird is laying eggs, leave the egg wherever the bird deposited it and wait to see if there are more. Most of the time a bird lays a clutch of eggs ranging from one or two for larger birds, to four or five for cockatiels. If you take the egg away right away, the bird's response will be "A predator got my egg, so I need to make another." As I said, this can be very stressful for Polly.

When she's finished producing her clutch, let Polly sit on the eggs for about seven days after the last one is laid, and then take them all away and reduce the amount of time she is exposed to sunlight—again, to about ten hours a day. She will think she has finished producing her clutch and should go about her regular daily affairs. Once this happens, Polly will typically return to her previous delightful self.

Sometimes, however, a bird will continue to lay eggs, one after another, until finally, after twenty-five eggs in one year, the frustrated owner calls me. The owner by now is upset, and the bird's body is worn out. This is the downside of providing Polly with a happy, healthy home. The environment encourages her body to make eggs, which she will keep doing until she raises a family. Once she has a family, however, it gives her something to do besides sit on eggs. She has to concentrate on raising a family now. And she typically won't produce more eggs until she's finished hatching and raising her first set of children. Therefore, the solution at this point is simpler than it seems.

If a bird won't quit laying eggs, find her a boy bird.

CHAPTER 6

Bye~Bye, Birdie:
Giving Polly up

You have delighted us long enough.

—JANE AUSTEN, *PRIDE AND PREJUDICE*

SOME RELATIONSHIPS JUST WON'T WORK.

Perhaps we rushed into a commitment without considering all the consequences. Or maybe some aspect of our lifestyle changed dramatically. In the best-case scenarios, those we love can evolve with us. But sometimes, that's impossible. Knowing when and how to say good-bye can prevent unnecessary pain for both parties.

Polly, for all her good intentions (and yours), might one day prove to be too much to handle. No matter how vigilantly you endeavor to understand your bird's psyche and to accommodate her idiosyncrasies, there's always the chance the bird will gain the upper hand. Or perhaps significant life changes will make your relationship impossible to continue. The reasons could be simple like a no-pets apartment, a new baby, or—heaven forbid—a bird-hating partner. At other times, however, Polly's biting, screaming, or sexual aggressiveness may disrupt an otherwise peaceful household. When that happens and every effort to correct the problems has been made, it's probably time to say farewell.

But giving up a pet can be incredibly painful for both bird and owner. To be reminded of that I need only to think of dear Mr. Duffey.

For almost four decades, Jesse was Mr. Duffey's closest confidant. They resided in Kensington, Maryland, where Mr. Duffey ran a small radio repair shop. Jesse was a big green boy, even by Amazon parrot standards. When he remembered to sit up straight, Jesse reached almost thirty-five centimeters in length, which put him head and shoulders above most birds in his class. Mr. Duffey was proud of Jesse and kept him in a cage at the repair shop where customers marveled at his bright yellow head and extroverted behavior.

Jesse had a large vocabulary which he exercised freely, particularly in the morning. "Top of the day to you," he would call. "Good morning, sunshine. Pretty bird. Pretty bird."

But idle chitchat was not his only appealing trait. He would ruffle his neck feathers and encourage customers to scratch his neck and if possible even rub a little under his wing or tail. Such behavior was so endearing that customers forgave the occasional swipe of Jesse's beak if they tickled a sensitive spot.

On holidays, Mr. Duffey and his wife, Chloe, would drive to the store and bring Jesse home to celebrate. After several years, the journey became something of a cherished tradition. Chloe sometimes wondered if Jesse felt frightened during the trip, but Mr. Duffey said he thought the bird liked looking out the window and seeing the streets, trees, and children rushing by.

"He doesn't get to see much inside the shop," he told Chloe. "I like to let him watch life pass by."

Nearly thirty-seven years passed in this comfortable fashion. Jesse was very much loved, and he loved well in return. Then Mr. Duffey's eyesight started to fail, and the tiny parts on the broken radios seemed to grow even smaller. Hurried customers began seeking help at bigger electronics stores. Mr. Duffey worried a bit, but Jesse remained his cheerful self, calling a hearty hello to anyone who stopped by. If times were changing, Jesse was unaware of it.

But then Mr. Duffey's wife passed away. Mr. Duffey tried to be strong. He believed in tradition, and so Jesse still came home for Christmas and New Year's Eve. During these lonely holidays, the two ate dinner together and celebrated as best they could. When Mr. Duffey said a prayer out loud for Chloe, Jesse often stopped chewing his birdseed and listened attentively. Mr. Duffey appreciated this gesture of respect.

Finally, however, continuing even small daily traditions proved too much for the aging gentleman. Mr. Duffey, then in his eighties, realized that financially and physically he could no longer run a business and maintain a home simultaneously. At the urging of friends, he and Jesse closed up the shop and moved into government-subsidized senior citizen housing. Before the relocation, he telephoned me for advice about uprooting Jesse.

I inquired about what his new neighbors were like. After all, in a close-knit high-rise, Jesse's morning ramblings might be unwelcome.

"I don't expect that'll matter too much," Mr. Duffey said. "If the other residents are like me, they're all hard of hearing anyway."

Mr. Duffey's new home was a small studio on the eleventh floor of the building. Given the apartment's size, there was no appropriate place for Jesse's cage except the center of the room. There the cage served as a divider of sorts, separating the bed from the living room. Every morning Mr. Duffey would try to read the newspaper and drink his coffee without waking Jesse. This was no small feat; the bird's hearing was sharp—unlike that of the neighbors—and he often awoke just moments after Mr. Duffey had brewed his first cup. Then Jesse's incessant talking would start. Jesse, accustomed to a steady stream of new faces in the radio repair store, now had only Mr. Duffey with whom to discuss the day's matters. This grew a bit wearisome, but Mr. Duffey tried to be patient. Jesse was his only companion.

Then one day, Mr. Duffey met Melinda.

Melinda lived just a few doors down from Mr. Duffey. They met one day in the hall when Melinda was complaining to a friend about a broken vacuum cleaner. Mr. Duffey, overhearing their conversation, volunteered that he was pretty handy with stubborn machines. He fixed Melinda's vacuum; she invited him over for spaghetti; and they became fast friends.

Unfortunately, Melinda was not enchanted with Jesse and his relentless coffee-talk. She thought the bird's noisy habits were much too disturbing for Mr. Duffey, who suffered from high blood pressure. Although their friendship was strictly platonic, Melinda spent a good deal of time at Mr. Duffey's apartment. About the same age, they played bridge together and enjoyed listening to Frank Sinatra albums. Often Jesse would interrupt their activities when he grew bored. The distraction upset Mr. Duffey, although he wouldn't admit it. But

Melinda noticed his distress and grew more and more convinced that the bird wasn't good for Mr. Duffey's health.

Melinda's suspicions were confirmed when Mr. Duffey's doctor admitted him into the local hospital for a two-day comprehensive cardiac evaluation and warned him to cut back on stress. While Mr. Duffey was away, Melinda cared meticulously for Jesse. But when she visited her friend in the hospital, Melinda was forthright: "Jesse needs to go. It's time," she told him. "You can't keep living like this."

Mr. Duffey at first was unbending; he couldn't imagine life without Jesse. They had lived together for almost forty years now. Mr. Duffey had no children, and Jesse in many ways was his only remaining link to his late wife. There was no way he could give Jesse up.

When he came home from the hospital, however, the morning strain of Jesse's calling continued to wear him down. He began phoning me once a week, then more frequently, asking what would happen to Jesse if he gave the bird up. I explained that I could keep Jesse for several weeks at Animal Exchange and then find him a new home. If Mr. Duffey changed his mind in the meantime, he could always take Jesse back.

Our talks continued for a couple of months until Mr. Duffey finally made the decision to part with Jesse. I drove to his apartment on a Monday and rode the elevator to the eleventh floor. Mr. Duffey answered the door after my first knock. His face was resigned and he looked tired, partly because Jesse had been waking up earlier these past few weeks as the days' length increased, but mostly because of the burden of his decision. He asked me to stay for a cup of coffee. His face was sad, almost pleading. I wanted to stay to comfort him, but I knew that would only prolong the painful good-bye, and so I politely declined.

When he introduced me to Jesse, I complimented him on the bird's excellent appearance, which was much better than I had expected, given Mr. Duffey's illness.

"I trim his toenails regularly," Mr. Duffey said. "Maybe you could, too? I think it keeps him happy." I nodded and agreed to do so.

After handing me a bag of Jesse's favorite birdseed, he helped me carry the cage down in the elevator and out to the car. Jesse, who probably figured he was going back to the shop or home for the holidays, climbed amicably onto his perch and stared out the window at Mr. Duffey. I bade Mr. Duffey good-bye and reminded him that if he changed his mind during the next few weeks he could always telephone. He nodded, but we both knew he wouldn't.

I started the car and pulled out of the driveway. Mr. Duffey watched us go, and when I glanced in the rearview mirror, I saw him still standing there. He waved and then bowed his head slightly before quickly rubbing one frail hand across his eyes. As for Jesse, he kept his footing on the perch and stared out the window, watching one long part of his own life fade into the past.

When making his decision to give Jesse up, Mr. Duffey did everything right. He thoroughly thought through the ramifications, considered his existing lifestyle—the tiny apartment and his own ill health—and solicited my help to ease the transition for Jesse and himself. (Jesse eventually was placed in a research project at the University of Maryland where they are studying the vocalization skills of Amazon parrots. He is well cared for and much loved by the students who adore his chattering.)

Owners are not always so diligent. Whether out of ignorance or pure frustration, they sometimes simply release the bird into the wild. That is absolutely the *worst* mistake an owner can make, not to mention that it is illegal to release a bird that is not native to this country. Think of how well you would fare if someone suddenly dropped you in the middle of a desert island with no boat, no real survival skills, and no food. Likewise, Polly's chances of surviving outdoors are slim. There are many predators lurking out there: other birds, cats, cars, and electrical wires. Don't put her through such trauma; most pet stores and humane societies will gladly accept a free unwanted bird. All it takes is one telephone call. For a bird you've loved for so long, and who has loved you back, it's worth the trouble.

CRYBABY POLLY

Owners most often relinquish their pet birds because some aspect of their life changes and the bird simply doesn't fit in. Often this isn't the bird's fault. If Polly has behaved well for ten years and suddenly begins yelling, biting, or kicking food, perhaps something in her environment has changed and is upsetting her. This could constitute something as basic as a relocation. Maybe she doesn't like the position of her cage by the big bay windows in your new house. (Remember, too much light can be *very* stimulating.) Or perhaps the new kitten you find so endearing is torturing the bird by switching its tail under her cage and making unsettling mewing noises.

Before jumping to conclusions about a bird's mental health and banishing her from the household, find out if a slight change in scenery or cage location will do the trick.

Sometimes, owners who have two birds of the same species would be better off with just one. I always tell customers: one bird for a pet, two for breeding. The individual bird that is focused solely on you, the owner, is the one that will learn to talk and can become a lifelong companion. If you own two cats or two dogs, think about how they romp across the house, chasing each other, causing disturbances they wouldn't necessarily make if they lived solo. Birds, too, can cause a tumult, even though they live in cages. If Polly has a friend, she's got someone with whom she can talk birdspeak, chase around, and even be romantic with. I know from customers' complaints that this can be *very* disturbing, and it's not necessarily what you had intended your pet relationship to be.

Some lifestyle transitions can make it impossible for owners to keep a bird. A job transfer overseas might leave no place for a bird in your life, or a new job might force you to travel extensively.

When I traveled in Australia for a month, my own cockatoo, Bill, was watched by a neighbor who truly enjoyed the opportunity to visit with my bird. At first things seemed normal when I returned from my trip. A week later, however, when Bill was outside of his cage, he reached out with his beak and tried to extract an ounce of flesh from my side as I passed by. I turned and looked at him—did *not* yell—and said, "I guess you didn't like me leaving you behind." Okay, so perhaps he didn't understand my words, but he recognized that I got the message: he was displeased with my leaving. I had clearly acknowledged Bill's unhappiness, and that was the last correction he imposed upon me.

More frequently, owners must give up their birds to accommodate someone else. One kind elderly lady named Anne Jones sadly relinquished her cockatiel to me after her granddaughter, who had asthma, came to stay with her. Cockatiels and cockatoos both have powdery patches on their feathers that will leave a film on your fingers when you pet them. This fine powder aggravated her granddaughter's asthma. Anne had little choice but to find another home for the bird, but that didn't make the farewell any less painful.

Mary, another one of my customers, had a different sort of problem with Bobbi, her Mexican red Amazon parrot. For two years, Bobbi was Mary's only child. When Bobbi was not out on her T-stand perch, she lived in a cage nestled between the foot of the staircase and the kitchen. Every morning while Mary packed her lunch for the day before heading to work, she would let Bobbi out to cruise about the kitchen.

Mary and her husband tried unsuccessfully for nearly a year to conceive a child. As her disappointment mounted, Mary grew closer to Bobbi, resigning herself to the fact that this sweet creature might be her only chance at parenthood. Sensing sadness, as animals sometimes can, Bobbi tried her best to make Mary feel loved.

In December, Mary's prayers were answered when her doctor phoned and told her she was pregnant. Throughout her nine months of carrying the child, Bobbi never wavered in her loyalty. When Mary would lie exhausted on the couch at the end of a day, Bobbi would sometimes sit on her stomach as Mary's hands felt for movement from her growing child. When Mary finally left on a Tuesday for the hospital, she was in too great a rush to say good-bye to Bobbi. But the parrot waited patiently at home for her return.

Several days later, Mary and her husband returned with their son, Franklin, who weighed in at a healthy eight pounds, five ounces. Bobbi was ecstatic about their return, although perhaps a little perplexed that Mary stayed upstairs so much instead of coming down for their usual morning rendezvous. Franklin, meanwhile, was testing out a set of very healthy lungs and demanding Mary's attention constantly. It took Bobbi only three days to notice that every time Franklin cried out in a violent scream, Mary came running. Well, Bobbi figured, what works for Franklin . . .

So Bobbi began mimicking Franklin's cries with such startling accuracy that Mary indeed came running, thinking her child needed attention, changing, or food. Bobbi was mightily pleased by this turn of events and very happy he'd discovered a surefire way of grabbing Mary's attention once again.

Mary, however, was less than pleased with Bobbi's shrewd behavior. Already exhausted from the constant attention the newborn required, she simply couldn't bear to awaken from a much-needed nap to the crying of her bird. She decided with much remorse that Bobbi would have to go.

Although Mary was very attached to her bird, she felt more attached to her baby. At her wit's end, she telephoned Animal Exchange and asked if I would take Bobbi. I did, and immediately found a new home without an infant. Bobbi attempted for a few months to solicit attention through baby cries and then reverted to her normal conversation and settled in nicely.

Such transitions can be smoothed with some careful planning. First, I always encourage owners to deliver birds in their original cages. A bird's cage is its castle, and when making a pilgrimage to a new home, the security of a familiar cage can truly ease any feeling of upheaval.

Moreover, familiar toys, ladders, climbing rings, and food should all be sent along for a bird to play with in its new environment, particularly early on while it's still adapting. Birds adjust well to new situations but the more continuity you provide, the less likely they are to fall into a funk.

I knew one parakeet whose owner was a classical pianist. When the owner started traveling on tour for longer stays, the parakeet came to the store where I found her a new home. The parakeet's new owners were sensitive enough to play some Beethoven at first to make the tiny bird feel safe and welcome. I applaud their sensitivity. However, don't make yourself miserable if you're a heavy metal buff and hate classical arrangements. Who knows? Polly might become a Metallica fan. I've known a few head-banging birds in my time. For adoptive parents, the object is to help a bird feel comfortable in a new environment without disrupting your own life.

WHO'S TO BLAME?

I never want customers to feel guilty about bringing unwanted pets to a local pet store. I find that letting go of a beloved pet is often much harder for the owner than it is for the bird because the owner must deal with his feelings of guilt. However, I have little sympathy for owners who don't carefully think through the ramifications of owning a bird *before* they buy one. Birds do talk, and they do make a mess, and they do sometimes bite. Purchasing a bird isn't like buying a fish, which will swim quietly with little ado. Birds take time and attention. We really want you to think of them as new family members.

So I was very displeased with the young man who appeared at Animal Exchange's doorstep with his parakeet only three months after taking him home.

"He talks too much," the young man complained. "I don't understand why he won't be quiet."

I sighed. "Now, I explained to you that these little birds like to chat. You told me you wanted a talking bird."

"I know, but I didn't realize how *much* he would talk," he continued. "No matter how often I tell him to shut up, he won't. In fact he now tells me to shut up."

I held my tongue and said we would find a new home for the parakeet. This man refused to relinquish the birdcage, however, insisting he wanted to buy a pair of "quieter" finches and needed the cage to house them. So I said I'd take the little bird to the back of the store and find him a new, suitable place to live. But when I reached into the cage to remove the bird, I noticed that his water was moving almost like the water in a tiny wave pool.

I took a closer look and saw that the water dish was packed with a swarm of mosquito wigglers—baby mosquitoes that had just hatched. That water dish was the foulest thing I had ever seen in a birdcage. Instead of cleaning the water dish each night, it appeared this guy had only added fresh water on top of the old. While the mosquitoes probably wouldn't have killed the bird, it's neither sanitary nor healthful for a tiny parakeet to drink water that's filled with squirming creatures. The mosquitoes' presence was further indication to me that this customer was totally unprepared for the rigors of pet parenthood.

I promptly put the parakeet into a clean cage in the back of the store. Then I hurried out to instruct his ex-owner on proper bird care. The young man had fled, however, leaving the filthy cage behind. He'd obviously noticed me discover the infested water dish and decided to spare himself a lecture.

I don't know if the parakeet talked so much because he had a natural gift for gab or because he was expressing his unhappiness about his living conditions. Regardless, it's imperative for owners to understand their responsibilities to a bird before making a full-time commitment. Similarly, it helps to ask yourself in advance how well you will be able to handle a bird's habits. A little soul-searching can prevent a breakup later on.

I find some of the toughest good-byes are between the elderly and their birds, like Mr. Duffey and Jesse. Unfortunately, they are the ones who often must say farewell sooner than expected. When senior citizens must leave their home for the additional services available at a nursing home or hospital, pets are rarely permitted to accompany them.

Since I met Elizabeth, however, I have never given up hope that a little patience and perseverance will solve what seems to be an overwhelming problem.

Elizabeth was a beautiful woman by almost any standards. Her slender figure still turned heads, even though she was nearly seventy years old. She had pure white hair, which she pulled off her square face into a loose cascade, but her most striking asset was her gray eyes, which shone with the wide-eyed energy of a teenager. Elizabeth's husband had died in an automobile accident when she was fifty-five. Their love had been pure and unspoiled, and Elizabeth never saw fit to remarry, although many a man had certainly tried.

I remember Elizabeth from the early days when Animal Exchange first opened. She had owned several birds over the years, but her final pet was a stunning green Senegal parrot with a golden belly. Elizabeth named the bird Antonia, after the heroine of Willa Cather's famous novel, *My Ántonia*.

Antonia wasn't much of a talker, but she was an inordinate source of comfort to her owner nonetheless. Elizabeth loved to read and would take Antonia out on the sun porch in the spring as she paged through that week's literary selection. Sometimes she would read Antonia passages aloud. Although she wasn't certain, Elizabeth thought the bird enjoyed Fitzgerald and Ibsen the most.

Elizabeth told me she doesn't remember when the passages in the books first started to blur. Perhaps it was during another reading of *A Doll House,* she said, although it might have been somewhere deep in *This Side of Paradise.* But one day Elizabeth realized that even with her reading glasses she was straining terribly to decipher the lines that brought her so much happiness.

Her doctors were frank. Severe macular degeneration was robbing Elizabeth of her eyesight. The condition was common for people her age, and unfortunately the doctors could do little to help her. With the rapid progression of the disease in her retinas, they predicted that Elizabeth would be completely blind within a year.

When she learned this, she began to make plans for her future and for Antonia's. Elizabeth lived in a grand old three-story Victorian house and was reluctant to stay there when she could no longer see the beautiful polished-oak banisters and intricate ceiling moldings that made her so proud of the home. Moreover, she believed there would come a day when she would no longer be able to maintain the home by herself. Always a practical woman, she arranged to move into special senior housing where a nurse was on call twenty-four hours a day.

Had the housing community permitted pets, Elizabeth certainly could have continued caring for Antonia. The blind are perfectly capable of providing outstanding care for birds. The community hadn't allowed pets for many years, however, and Elizabeth approached me about taking Antonia.

"It's the hardest thing I've ever had to do, Ruth," she told me slowly. Her piercing gray eyes were clouded that day, and it pained me to look at her. "But I know I can count on you to find Antonia a good home."

I promised that Antonia would be safe with us until I found her a loving new owner. When the day finally arrived for Elizabeth to drop Antonia off for good, she arrived promptly at 4:00 P.M., just before the store closed. By this time Elizabeth could no longer drive, and I went out to help them as soon as her taxi pulled up. We found Antonia a comfortable space in the back of the store, away from the hustle and bustle around the cash register.

After helping the bird settle in, Elizabeth turned toward Antonia. She pressed one slender hand against the birdcage and gave a small sigh. "One day we'll read *Gatsby* together again," she whispered to the bird. "So I won't say good-bye now. Be good for Ruth."

And with those words, she left Antonia and returned to the waiting taxi.

For weeks afterward I made no attempt to find Antonia a new home. In fact, I went so far as to tell interested customers that she wasn't for sale. Something inside me couldn't bear to let the bird leave the store. I felt that she somehow still belonged with Elizabeth. My staff thought I was crazy, but I had a nagging feeling that it would be wrong to give Antonia up.

One day I decided to visit Elizabeth. She was in good spirits and had made herself a lovely home at the senior community. She was able to order books on tape, which made her predicament slightly more bearable.

We talked for a while, and she confessed that she still missed Antonia every day. "She was so wonderful to have around," Elizabeth told me. "She didn't say much, but I always knew she was there for me. I could still take care of her. I know I could."

Seeing how orderly and immaculate she kept her new home, I didn't doubt her words. As I was leaving that day, I ran into one of the nurses. We stopped and chatted for a moment, and the nurse asked me how Elizabeth seemed. I told her how pleased I was that she was adjusting so well to her new home. "I just wish she could see Antonia," I said ruefully.

The nurse looked puzzled. "Who's Antonia?"

I explained, in more detail than she probably wanted to hear, how close Elizabeth and her parrot had been. I described their reading sessions and how much I thought they missed each other. Then I looked at my watch and realized I was late for an appointment at the store.

The nurse looked at me thoughtfully as we said good-bye. Two days later she called Animal Exchange. "I've arranged something special with the executive director here," she told me. "Although we really do discourage pets here, we've made a few exceptions in the past. The director says that if you will make certain Elizabeth can properly care for Antonia, the bird can join her here."

That weekend I packed up Antonia's few possessions and loaded her into my car. I arrived at Elizabeth's door as the sun was setting. She was sitting in a rocker on her porch listening to an audiotaped book. I called to her so she would know I was approaching.

"Ruth, I'm so glad you came," she said, fumbling to turn off the tape recorder. "Come here so I can give you a hug."

I set the cage down beside her chair, glad at that moment that Antonia wasn't talkative and wouldn't ruin the surprise.

"Elizabeth," I said, "I have a surprise for you."

She looked in my direction with curiosity. I carefully lifted Antonia out of the cage.

"Hold out your hand, Elizabeth."

She did, and without any prodding, Antonia stepped from my finger to Elizabeth's.

For a moment, this beautiful woman did not move. Then she slowly and tenderly touched Antonia's soft face. With her voice quavering, ever so slightly, she asked, "You brought my Antonia for a visit, Ruth?"

"No, Elizabeth, she's here to stay." And I explained what the kind nurse had done for her. As I did, her gray eyes shone.

We went inside to help Antonia settle in. As I watched them together, rejoicing in their reunion, I thought how nice it was to know that some good-byes didn't have to be forever.

CHAPTER 7

Freebird:

Letting Polly fly the coop

But though my wing is closely bound,
My heart's at liberty;
My prison walls cannot control
The flight, the freedom of the soul.

—JEANNE GUYON,
"A PRISONER'S SONG"

FOR THOSE WHO ARE UNAWARE OF THE
dangers of flying, the sight of an airborne bird might inspire
thoughts of simple elegance, sweet summer breezes, and complete freedom and joy.

I, however, think of boiling spaghetti sauce, whirling ceiling fan blades, and hungry hawks.

Flying can be a hazardous and even a deadly pastime for
pet birds. This is why I strongly urge all my customers to clip
their birds' wing feathers—a simple, painless procedure that
prevents the bird from flying any great distance. In nature,
birds need to fly for very specific reasons, the most important
being their need to obtain food and avoid predators. As an
owner, you will fulfill these needs for your bird. Therefore,

there is no good reason for Polly to fly and many, *many* good reasons why she should not.

A BIRD IN THE PAN IS . . .
IN A LOT OF PAIN

The way she remembers it, Mrs. Georgia Spate was in a fine mood that particular Friday afternoon. She was expecting company for supper at around 6:00 P.M., and by 4:30 she already had set the table, buttered the French bread to go in the oven, and mixed the ingredients for her special spaghetti sauce. There was plenty of time left to bathe, dress, and greet her guests.

Plenty of time, that was, until she let Sidney out.

Do you remember what killed the cat? Well, Sidney was a curious cockatiel. Mrs. Spate hung fascinating toys in his cage, but Sidney was always more interested in what was on the other side of the bars. Each day as Mrs. Spate tidied up the house, moving from room to room with vacuum and broom, Sidney would call for her—quietly at first, and then with greater urgency.

Eventually Mrs. Spate would give in and release Sidney from his cage, and he would promptly fly to his favorite spots in the room, which included a lampshade and the top of the drapes. As he explored, Sidney talked about his findings in language Mrs. Spate had taught him: "Hello, hello! What's this? Oh, my darling!"

Typically he was remarkably well behaved, waiting until he returned to the cage to deposit droppings and rarely chewing anything of great value.

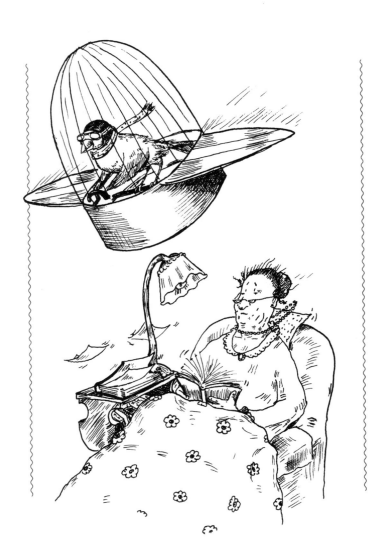

The afternoon of the dinner party, Sidney had worked himself into a panic watching Mrs. Spate bustle about. She hadn't had time to let him out yet, and like most animals, he could sense that a special event of some sort was about to take place. He wasn't sure what it was; he only knew he didn't want to be left out of the festivities. So he fussed and fussed until Mrs. Spate emerged from the kitchen, wiping her hands on her apron.

"Yes, my darling. Yes, Sidney," she cooed. "Everything's fine. Do you need Mommy to let you out for a bit?"

Sidney danced back and forth on his perch, head down. That meant yes. He pressed his tiny plump yellow body against the door and pecked the latch with his beak.

Mrs. Spate opened the cage, and Sidney flew out immediately. He had much to examine that day and wanted to start promptly. He immediately began darting about the living room, checking to see what had changed since his last adventure. Mrs. Spate watched him for a moment, and because the bird seemed completely preoccupied, she returned to the kitchen to heat up the spaghetti sauce before heading upstairs to dress for the party. With the stove's fan running, she didn't hear the flapping of wings behind her neck, and she didn't see the curious Sidney until he landed with a plop in the sauce. Fortunately the sauce had just begun to bubble around the edges and was still cold on top, so Sidney didn't cook his goose.

Still, this wasn't a good situation.

As Sidney sank deeper into the sea of red tomato chunks and green peppers, Mrs. Spate watched, stunned for a moment, before crying out, "Oh, Sidney!" Sidney, for once, didn't have much to say. He tried to flap, but the sauce was thick—Mrs. Spate's husband favored it that way—and the bird's efforts were in vain. So he looked helplessly at Mrs. Spate as his body disappeared slowly into the stew.

Before the bird sank completely, Mrs. Spate gathered her senses, removed the pot from the stove, and quickly carried the sauce and her bird to the sink. There she dumped her afternoon's work down the drain, grabbing a stunned Sidney as he came pouring out with a small bay leaf stuck in one wing.

The time was now 5:10 P.M. Poor Mrs. Spate had an unscathed, but dirty bird, no spaghetti sauce, and six guests arriving for dinner in less than an hour. She was no longer in a fine mood.

Sidney, who had thought the bubbling sauce looked interesting and had flown in for a closer peek, wasn't seriously harmed. Birds' feathers insulate them—to a certain extent and for a short time—from extreme temperatures, both hot and cold. The sauce was greasy, however, and oil doesn't easily rinse off birds' feathers with plain water—as we learned after the *Exxon Valdez* oil spill in Alaska and the Tampa Bay catastrophe in August of 1993. In both of those horrific instances, it took cases of detergent donated by companies like Procter & Gamble and Colgate-Palmolive to clean the black goo from the feathers and eyes of the local seagulls, pelicans, egrets, and great blue herons.

For Sidney, it took a washing in a mild detergent. Mrs. Spate finished just as her guests pulled into the driveway. Sidney was bathed and feeling much better, although he smelled vaguely like oregano. Mrs. Spate, on the other hand, was still dressed in sweatpants and feeling quite irritated. However, a good story can often rescue an endangered social situation, and Mrs. Spate certainly had one to tell.

Sidney's wings, needless to say, had not been clipped, and his flying had gotten him into hot water, literally and figuratively. His story had a happy ending, but many others do not.

I remember the parakeet who was intrigued by the sizzling sound of bacon in a frying pan and landed in the pan feetfirst. The pan had a nonstick surface, which was to the parakeet's advantage, but the bird's toes weren't protected by feathers, and the hot grease burned them badly. In this case, the veterinarian was unable to save the bird. Both feet had been destroyed, and the bird had to be put to sleep.

Be very careful about letting a bird fly about when you are using the stove or the garbage disposal and even when you're chopping onions with a butcher knife. Kitchens can be unfriendly places for birds.

If you still aren't convinced that flying is a dangerous pastime, consider these avian mishaps, which can be gruesome. I've known too many birds who have lost a leg or a wing to a ceiling fan or a door. One gentle lovebird I knew flew up to examine a spinning ceiling fan and, horribly, was decapitated. Another customer shut her underwear drawer too fast and caught her cockatiel's leg in the crack. The veterinarian was forced to amputate the limb. Moreover, there are horrible incidents of clueless birds flying headfirst into freshly polished windows and breaking their necks.

As if the indoor risks aren't great enough, the outside world presents its own set of pitfalls. Many people believe their bird loves them *so* much that it will never leave. After carrying a nuzzling lovebird around on their shoulder inside, they figure it's safe to step onto the porch with Polly still attached. "After all," they say, "she's never left me before." Of course she hasn't. It only happens once.

Think of your pet as a jailbird: escape is always foremost on his mind. I remember a middle-aged man who entered the attached garage to throw out the garbage one evening. He never saw the family's parakeet follow him. The man's son had just left in his car, and the garage door was still raised. Before the man could reach the button to close the door, the startled bird slipped out and disappeared into the night.

When this happens, the fire department is typically unsuccessful in rescuing birds from high places and reluctant to try. Unlike a cat, who will just sit petrified, a bird will fly higher to get away from the scary red fire engine and the big man who begins climbing up the tree while the neighbors gape. And when the bird reaches the highest branches, it will likely fly somewhere else altogether.

Once she is gone, it's unlikely you'll ever see Polly again. The outside world, even in a white-picket-fence community, might as well be the jungle for a small pet bird. The perils are great because Polly sticks out like a sore thumb. Your bird, who might have viewed dogs and cats as her friends, will discover that's not necessarily the case once she's outside the safe confines of her cage. Moreover, a bright-colored, naive little bird flapping aimlessly through the backyard can make a tasty snack for a hungry hawk or come to tragedy in the path of a speeding car.

Pet birds often have trouble finding food in the wild because they are accustomed to being served by a personal chef—you. They may find their way to a bird feeder, which will satisfy their appetite if the seed is a type they find tasty. But the exposure puts them at risk in two ways: bigger birds or other pets might find them easy targets, or a neighbor might decide to capture and keep Polly. A lot of people acquire new pets by picking up lost or stray animals. Chances are, neither option is particularly appealing to the original owner.

I've had customers who liked to let their bird loose in the car while they were driving. They couldn't imagine what possible mischief a bird could get into in an automobile. But what if they wreck the car and Polly gets hurt or goes flying out a broken window? This happens more often than you might expect, because the driver can be easily distracted by a loose bird fluttering about the car.

Moreover, ambulance crews are typically reluctant to carry animals to the hospital along with a human patient. I knew a woman who after a rather severe auto accident simply refused to get out of her crumpled car unless her sun conure could accompany her to the hospital. Her bird had been sitting in a carrier—with its door open—when she crashed, and the woman feared that the tow-truck driver would not know what to do with the conure. Valuable treatment time was wasted as she argued with the medics, but she held firm until they conceded and loaded the bird back into its cage.

The woman faced another confrontation at the hospital when the staff refused to allow the bird to come inside. Ultimately, a nurse who owned a pet bird herself intervened and kept the wreck victim's conure safe in its cage until the owner was treated and could leave.

You might not be so fortunate. Always keep your bird in his cage with the door latched when you are in the car, even if his wings are clipped. Like a child's car seat, a cage will offer some protection for the bird if you crash. Also remember that if you roll down a window and your bird isn't caged, you will have absolutely no way to prevent his escape.

One woman stopped traffic for forty-five minutes when her parakeet flew out of an open window of her car at a major intersection. The woman panicked, jumped from her car, and chased the bird until it perched atop a stoplight. She stayed there in the middle of the intersection until a policeman finally ordered her to move. Then she called the fire department on her cellular phone, but they were short-staffed and refused to leave the station to rescue a bird. So the woman sat on the side of the road, just watching her parakeet. Unfortunately, the bird never moved, and when darkness fell, the woman lost track of her parakeet forever. Tempting though it may be to have the bird loose in the car with you, safety dictates that you keep your feathered friend safely confined.

THE PREVENTION:
A LITTLE TRIM WILL DO IT

These frightful tales don't mean that you can never let a bird out of the cage. On the contrary, if a parrot is to establish itself as a proper member of the family, direct interaction is important. Moreover, part of the joy of bird ownership, particularly with bigger species, is removing the creatures from their cage, stroking and bathing them, and showing them off to visitors.

Clipping a bird's wing feathers is like cutting human hair—it doesn't hurt, and after the bird molts, the new feathers will need to be clipped again. I teach my customers how to do this at home. Any pair of sharp scissors will work, provided you can easily wield them. Typically you must restrain a bird by holding him with a towel or a net. Spread the bird's wing so you can clearly see each feather.

A bird's wing is constructed in basically the same design as our arm. The outermost part, which holds the long primary-flight feathers, is like our hand. The middle section has long feathers called secondaries and corresponds to our forearm. Both primary and secondary feathers are covered at the base by covert feathers. The tips of these covert feathers provide a convenient guideline for trimming the long flight feathers so the bird will be able to break its fall but not gain altitude when it tries to fly.

When a feather is growing, it has a blood supply. This makes it red in the middle. People often get hysterical at the idea of cutting a "blood" feather and causing it to bleed. The best way to avoid this is always to trim the primary and secondary feathers out beyond the coverts. That way you won't hit a new, freshly growing feather, which is shorter and still has a blood supply attached. The wings will need to be trimmed again when the cut feathers fall out and are replaced by new ones. This happens about twice a year.

Many people trim both wings, but I recommend trimming just one. This will keep the bird slightly off-balance if it tries to fly. When the feathers begin to grow in, if both wings are trimmed symmetrically, the bird will just try harder to fly and may gather enough speed to injure itself or get into mischief. Moreover, a bird who is a little off-balance is much less interested in flying and more dependent on you. This often translates into a better-behaved bird.

THE WIND BENEATH THEIR WINGS

A word of warning: even if their wings are trimmed, birds can get into trouble, particularly outside. I've known many a tiny lovebird with clipped wings who got caught in an updraft of the wind and went soaring into another part of the yard or across the street. Be very careful about taking your bird outside, clipped wings or not.

If Polly gets loose, there are some tricks to getting her back, but most of them are anecdotal, and success is not guaranteed. These techniques have worked for some bird owners I know, but each bird is different. The more aware you are of your pet's likes and dislikes, the better you will perform in a rescue situation.

I think of this next tale as a tribute to perseverance. Klee was a lovely half-moon sun conure who was deeply attached to Schuyler, her owner. Schuyler and Klee, who lived next to a nature preserve, would often sit on the patio together—Klee in her cage and Schuyler on his artist's stool. A lawyer by profession, Schuyler painted as a hobby and often relaxed at day's end by capturing images of the preserve. As the sun set, Schuyler would fill his canvas with bold colors and listen to the wild birds calling in the distance. Klee would watch Schuyler's brush moving rhythmically over the canvas and cock her head curiously each time she heard an interesting cry from the preserve.

One late afternoon when Schuyler was preparing to grill a steak, he released Klee from her cage. He had just given her a bath in her favorite dish, where she would toss water back into her feathers and fluff them up. Schuyler never thought his sun conure would leave him, and Klee—whose wings weren't clipped—probably had no intention of leaving. But when Schuyler lit the grill, the flames startled her, and she panicked and took off for the nearest tree in the nature preserve. Schuyler spent the rest of the afternoon trying to coax her down, but to no avail. When night fell, he carefully marked the tree that held his dear Klee by placing a big stick on the ground at its base.

The next morning he stayed home from work and went back to the tree, where he continued calling to the bird.

"Klee, please come down," he said. "I really need to go to the office." The sun conure looked at him with some interest but stayed put. Schuyler refused to leave her, despite the growing number of neglected clients he knew were leaving angry messages on his answering machine.

His vigilant but exhausting watch continued for four days as Klee flew from tree to tree occasionally, while Schuyler followed. On the fourth day he took Klee's bath dish with him into the preserve and set it near the tree. Klee took one look at the familiar dish and immediately flew down to enjoy a much-needed bath. A weary Schuyler took her home and, the next morning, brought her to Animal Exchange for a long-overdue wing-clipping.

In this instance, the sight of the dish inspired Klee's return. You can use the same strategy by setting out your bird's cage, her favorite toy, or her food dish. Anything that is familiar and comforting could entice your bird down from a high place. One woman accidentally capitalized on a stray bird's fascination with the color red during her efforts to lure him from a tree. The bird had escaped from its previous home. This woman saw him arrive in her yard and hoped she'd found a new pet.

Luckily this woman had recently purchased a cage in anticipation of buying a bird. She placed the cage in the middle of the yard where the stray bird could see it, but the bird stayed put. So she put a red apple in the cage, thinking maybe the bird was hungry. One look at the brilliant shiny object was all it took: the curious creature immediately left his perch in the tree and flew down into the cage for a closer look. *Slam!* The woman shut the cage door and took the bird inside. The coincidence was great for her, but probably not so good for a bereft owner somewhere else.

Sometimes seeing a familiar bird will bring Polly home, particularly if she and the other bird have been caged together. Just be careful not to lose two birds in one afternoon.

I've known a few owners who captured their escaped bird by playing music that the bird frequently heard inside the house. One man who often sang in the shower with his bird belted out the Gershwin tune "I've Got a Crush on You" in his driveway to woo his loose parakeet. The bird heard the familiar tune and darted down to perch on his shoulder. The neighbors were probably annoyed by the man's serenade, but at least he got his bird back.

If all else fails, the wet bird trick may produce results. Birds cannot easily fly if their wings are waterlogged. A woman in Bethesda, Maryland, was left in charge of an Amazon parrot when its owner, her sister, went to Europe on vacation. The day after the sister left, the bird flew out the door and perched in a tree. The hysterical woman called my store. We suggested she try to get close enough to soak the bird with a garden hose. She did—taking care not to turn the jet on full force—and showered the creature with watery drops. Sure enough, the startled bird tried to fly, but his wings were so wet that he simply plopped to the ground.

No matter where you live, you must constantly monitor a bird's flight patterns. It always pains me to recall the horrible accident that occurred at one college in Florida. A group of four female students living together there did a pretty good job of raising an enchanting little lovebird named Budweiser. They thought this name fit their lifestyle well at the time. As it turned out, Budweiser's name proved altogether too appropriate.

The bird was always allowed out and about in the apartment when the girls were home. It was their senior year, and studying wasn't particularly high on their agenda. One Saturday night they threw a rowdy bash, crowding about fifty beer-guzzling students into the tiny apartment. The music was blasting, people were dancing on the tables, and the din was nearly deafening.

Budweiser, whom everyone affectionately called Bud-Bird and who was outside his cage as usual, was a little disturbed by all the racket. His wings hadn't been trimmed recently and so he was easily able to hop and flap his way to the front door, which was wide open.

There on the porch, just beside the door, sat a blue cooler filled with ice and cold cans of beer. It was summer, and the ice had already begun to melt into a watery mess in the cooler because the reveling students kept forgetting to shut the lid. Budweiser slipped outside without anyone noticing him. Perhaps looking for a safe spot to rest, he flew into the cooler and landed in the melting water. No sooner had he done so than someone accidentally shut the lid and sat on the cooler for the next twenty minutes.

Surprisingly, no one wanted a drink in that time, which was very unfortunate for the bird. When the next person wanted a beer, he reached inside the cooler and found a Budweiser—but not the type he wanted. The bird had drowned among the aluminum cans, unable to scramble to safety in the chilly water. Needless to say, the party ended on a very unhappy note when the hosts were shown the tiny body.

The message in the bottle, so to speak, is that letting a bird out of its cage is always risky, particularly if they aren't properly monitored. I tell my customers there's a lesson in the tragedy of Bud-Bird: Birds that fly often die.

CHAPTER 8

Polly on Prozac?
Handling random peculiarities and passions

To define true madness
What is't but to be nothing else but mad?

—WILLIAM SHAKESPEARE, *HAMLET*

I'VE OWNED MORE THAN ONE HUNDRED birds since 1949, and between the store and my home, I've probably cared for thousands more. But not a month passes that doesn't find me listening to a fresh quirky tale from some bird owner whose pet has behaved in a most extraordinary manner. Just when I think I've heard it all, someone will tell me how her parakeet chews the covers of *Vogue* and *Harper's Bazaar* but won't touch *The New Yorker* or *The Economist.* Or an owner will say that when she went on a diet her sun conure flew to the top of the unused microwave every night and called "Ding-ding-ding," mimicking the noise the oven makes when food is ready. Obviously the bird had no intention of going the Slim Fast route as a gesture of solidarity.

Sometimes there are ready explanations for such behavior, many of which I've tried to outline in these chapters. For some outrageous bird conduct, however, I can only shrug and say, "If no one's getting hurt, don't fix what ain't broken." Other times I point to our own actions as human beings to make comparisons.

Sigmund Freud once said, "Analogies prove nothing, that is quite true, but they can make one feel more at home."

And indeed, students in my parrot psychology classes always seem to feel better when they realize their aviary travails aren't unique. Listening to stories about someone else's battles is like group therapy. "You aren't alone out there," I remind them. Here are some of their stories from over the years, along with any recommendations or guidance provided.

OBSESSIVE-COMPULSIVE BEHAVIOR

At night my bird, Sylvester, will enter his cage only if I hold a man's white undershirt in front of the cage door. Why is that?

Let's venture back to the bird's childhood. It's likely that this type of shirt somehow was imprinted early in Sylvester's memory. Perhaps when he was a chick, white diapers were used in his incubator or to catch the poop when he was being hand-fed. It's also possible that Sylvester associates the shirt with entering his cage because his previous owners draped an undershirt over the cage in the evening.

Since parrots are hole nesters, they routinely like to snuggle into enclosed spaces. The undershirt may give this fellow a feeling of security, much as a cage cover does when you settle a bird for the night.

And of course it's always possible that this behavior began with his mother, particularly if as a baby he was nourished by his biological mother and not hand-fed by a human. Is Sylvester white? Was his mother white? I'm not suggesting anything like an Oedipus complex, mind you, only that perhaps he connects the shirt with his mother who symbolizes safety in his mind.

Whatever the case, if it works, go with it. Many bird owners struggle to get their free-spirited birds to return to their cages. If it takes a man's undershirt, so be it. I just hope it's a clean one.

I love to wear jewelry, but my macaw seems to love it too much. He's always pulling at my rings and earrings. I'm scared he'll swallow them.

You're right to be concerned. Jewelry is fascinating to birds. It's attractive, it sparkles, and it bears a resemblance to seed in a bird's mind. Birds love to wedge their tongues in between a stone and its setting and explore the grooves. Their tongues have strong muscles, however, as do their beaks—and a bird's mouth can work like a jeweler's tool. I know too many birds who have managed to loosen lovely diamonds from rings and necklaces and then swallow or drop them. My entire staff can sometimes be found crawling around on the floor searching for a precious gem that some pick-pocketing Polly pried from a customer's jewelry. We try very hard to intercept problems before they occur, but birds are quick.

One cockatiel breeder who frequents my store lost the stone from her engagement ring this way. During a feeding session, she realized too late that a baby bird playing with her ring had swallowed the diamond. Bad luck for her indeed, but not so terrible for the bird. Birds need gravel in their gizzards to help grind up seeds, which they swallow in whole kernels. Wild birds will eat stones from your driveway; pet stores sell special gravel for house birds. Diamonds are incredibly hard, which makes them ideal for grinding seed.

With such a treasure locked inside him, this particular baby cockatiel didn't need to replace his grit for some time. And even though the breeder searched the baby's droppings for weeks, she never found the stone. Finally she sold the bird and told the lucky new bird owner to keep looking for a special gift, which came free with the purchase.

My bird is obsessed with bells, and rings them incessantly. I know she's just playing, but the sound can be very annoying.

Birds can become fixated on one individual toy, and a bell is particularly pleasing to them because it makes a noise. Chances are, too, that the owners might yell, "Be quiet, Polly," when the bell sounds too frequently. That sort of attention is a bonus in a bird's mind.

Sometimes birds will become oddly possessive of their toys. Wilson was a mild-mannered eighteen-year-old Amazon parrot whose one vice was the shiny bell hanging in his cage, which he abused with great regularity. Unfortunately, Wilson believed every bell in the household belonged to him.

At Christmastime, the family hung sleigh bells over the front door. Wilson promptly flew over to the door, established an outpost under the bells, and defended them against all newcomers. Because the family needed to use the door, the bells were removed and while the owner was carrying them away, Wilson chased her and attacked her feet. Bells are no longer used during the Christmas season at Wilson's home.

EATING DISORDERS

My bird, Cleo, sits at the table every night with me, and every time I take a bite of food, she eats some birdseed. But when I take a sip of water, she leaves the table and flies to the kitchen sink. This is very disruptive at dinnertime. What should I do?

Let's recall the flock concept. Remember, birds consider you a part of their flock. When the flock goes to feed, all members typically eat simultaneously. I suggested to this particular client that if she was tired of the interruptions at the dinner table she ought to place a small cup of water beside the bird's food dish. It was, I agreed, rather impolite for the bird to continually jump up from the table.

She tried the trick, and indeed Cleo was quite satisfied. Now the bird sips water from her own dish whenever her owner swallows from her glass. I warn bird owners that pets often become too sensitive to human eating patterns. While sharing a meal is a wonderful bonding experience between people and their birds, it can make a bird's eating habits rather dysfunctional. If you're on a starvation diet for the New Year, don't let your bird follow suit. Birds often imitate our eating patterns, and they can live without food for only a few days.

If you go out to dinner, and your bird is accustomed to eating with you, be certain later to sit with your bird and at least socialize with her while she feeds. The bird doesn't understand the concept of dining out and will wait for you. Likewise, when bird owners plan to go on vacation I always encourage them to tell their bird-sitters about any odd eating habits Polly might have.

This mealtime mimicking can have strange results, especially since birds like to use tools to imitate human actions whenever they can. Yo Yo the cockatoo, for example, insisted on eating my daughter's waffles from a fork, but he preferred to eat cereal from a spoon. After watching my daughter Lynn's eating patterns for years, Yo Yo had apparently developed his own sense of proper table manners.

> *I set a special place for my bird at the table, but he always wants to eat off of my plate.*

Some birds are a little more codependent than others, which can make them extremely high-maintenance. In some instances, giving them their own place setting isn't enough. Have you ever gone out to dinner with someone who ordered his own meal but spent most of the evening eyeing what was on your plate? The grass is always greener, the meat better prepared, the bread softer . . . In other words, Polly wants what you're eating because she thinks it might be tastier than what she's got, even if it's exactly the same meal. She likes the way you push peas about with a fork and how vigorously you slice your meat. That's where the action is at the dinner table. She also just wants to be closer to you.

One customer, Mr. Edwards, wanted a bird for years, but his wife always said "No way." It wasn't until Mrs. Edwards permanently left her husband that he fulfilled his avian fantasy. I believed Mr. Edwards missed his wife dearly and that was why he continued to set a place for her every night at the table. He then expected his perky Amazon parrot to fill the spot. But no matter how much he pleaded, the bird wouldn't eat from Mrs. Edwards's plate. No, no, the bird only wanted to nibble from Mr. Edwards's dinner, which was never enough for them both. I suggested to Mr. Edwards that he couldn't expect the parrot to be a substitute for his wife, particularly if he wanted any kind of real future with his bird. If the bird wanted to share his food, I thought he ought to let her.

Finally he solved the dilemma by fixing one bigger plate for them both. A fine start to a healthy relationship, I thought.

Why does my bird feed me corn from its mouth?

By regurgitating food, a bird is expressing affection toward you. Think about how a man might take a woman out for a nice dinner. By paying, he's trying to prove he can take care of her. Your bird is doing the same thing when it regurgitates food into your hand; a well-bonded bird often courts its owner this way.

Sometimes birds go overboard when it comes to their feeding patterns. Vinnie the parakeet lives in Tennessee where his owners furnish him with a cage full of fine toys, all of which he loves dearly. When Vinnie is out and about, he periodically darts back to his cage every so often to make certain his toys are safe. In fact, Vinnie is so concerned about his possessions that sometimes he will leave the dinner table to feed his toys a morsel of mashed potato or green beans. Vinnie's owners pretend this is perfectly normal, and kindly clean up the leftovers when Vinnie is finished.

If my canary gets to the table before me, he will consume an entire stick of butter. Is that healthy?

Birds develop favorite foods, just as we do, and sometimes these favorites are peculiar at best. Eating some butter won't hurt the bird, although an entire stick might be a little excessive for such a small stomach. A very congenial cockatiel used to come to Animal Exchange regularly for wing and nail grooming. The bird was healthy, but he always arrived with very sticky feathers. It turned out the bird was a pasta lover, but he would eat noodles only if they were doused with a delicate margarine spread. The bird would then play in the pasta and end up with greasy feathers. This was fine, although I encouraged the owner to give him frequent baths during the winter so the bird could properly fluff his feathers for insulation.

Bird diets vary mightily, and the creatures can handle a tremendous variety of cuisine. They generally don't overeat and usually should have food available all the time. Rarely have I seen instances of birds growing too fat.

When an older bird comes into the store for boarding, I often inquire about the diet. One of the most intriguing regimens I ever followed was for Ata, an African gray parrot who came to the United States with his State Department owners, who had purchased him as a baby in the Congo. Ata's staple diet was Spanish rice and Vienna sausages, and the bird looked great. I must admit, however, that I grew a bit weary of preparing this cuisine every morning during Ata's stay.

Like humans, birds have favorite treats. My mother brings grapes for her lunch whenever she visits the store. When Andy, my hyacinth macaw, hears the rattle of my mother's lunch bag, he immediately starts calling "Hello! Hello!" Mother knows he wants grapes, and she generously shares hers.

Some birds will even take a sip of your morning coffee; just know that if the birds are white, they'll probably need a bath afterward. And be careful about handling birds after they eat certain foods. Katie, my kakariki, had a particularly fiery beak after munching on red peppers—her favorite snack, for some inexplicable reason. If you are into kissing your bird, the burning sensation can be startling. Also, it's a bit awkward explaining to strangers that the red marks on your neck come from a bird's loving nibble.

> *My bird refuses to eat from a regular dish in his cage, instead demanding that I feed him from three tiny cups next to his perch. Constantly refilling his cups is a very time-consuming chore.*

This bird had his owner wrapped around his beak. He had trained her to fill those cups constantly throughout the day, and he took great pleasure in her attention. The bird refused to dine on anything placed lower because, of course, higher is always better. Moreover, the bird loved the constant interaction with his owner. What the owner thought was cute initially—those three little cups—fast became a dreary chore.

I advised her to remove the three tiny cups and place one bigger cup at a lower level in the cage. The bird balked for a day at this change, but eventually resigned himself to using the lower cup. It helped that this owner continued returning to the cage to soothe her bird and let him know that she wouldn't ignore him. When the bird realized his owner's presence wasn't directly linked to the three tiny cups, he had no problem eating from the bigger cup.

WHY ASK WHY?

My cockatoo lifts my eyelids with her beak when I'm sleeping. It wakes me up.

Yes, I would imagine it would. My first suggestion to this client, not to belabor the obvious, was to suggest putting the cockatoo in her cage during nap time. But let's look at why this bird behaved in such a peculiar way.

Actually, the bird was very smart. It's no fun to play alone. So when the bird grew bored with entertaining herself, she immediately decided to wake her only playmate.

Birds recognize our eyes as points of communication. This bird knew that in order to communicate with her owner, she needed to make eye contact. Small children will behave much the same way with sleeping parents, tugging at their arms, or prying open their eyelids.

Why does my bird hate men?

I hear this type of comment a lot. Sometimes a man-hating bird is responding to an individual who is uncomfortable around the bird, but more often than not the bird is competing for attention. Birds can be jealous of new individuals—and that could be a new boyfriend. Additionally, women frequently are the ones who feed the bird and clean its cage; therefore the bird views a husband, a boyfriend, or a male pal as a rival for the woman's attention. The bird's response in these situations is to bite the man and draw attention back to himself. You can mitigate this bias by persuading the men in your household to spend more quality time with the bird.

THE COMFORT ZONE

Polly seems lifeless. I've given her many toys, but she seems interested in none of them. She just sits quietly on her perch, not moving for much of the day.

Don't crowd your bird. She needs adequate space to move about and exercise her wings and muscles. It's possible she has too many toys in her cage, which can be both confusing and confining. Instead of playing, the bird is sitting dormant, afraid to move for fear she will bop her head on her swing or her dangling bell.

Once a customer arrived with a little blue parakeet whose cage was so packed with toys that he could barely squeeze between his perches. When he bumped into a toy, the owner thought he was enjoying himself, so she would add more toys. We finally persuaded her to rotate the toys, leaving only two or three in the cage at any one time. This was bound to make life more comfortable and intellectually stimulating for the bird.

Many people put their birds into round cages for decorative appeal. This may be aesthetically pleasing to you, but it's no good for the bird, particularly one with a long tail and wings. A round cage can seriously limit the amount of space a bird can use. A rectangular cage of comparable size provides a much more comfortable floor plan. Save the round cage for potted ivy or other plants and treat your bird to a boxier space big enough for him to spread his wings.

Can I potty-train my bird?

Many owners learn to anticipate when their bird will make a dropping. The bird may step backward and wiggle its tail, or she may ruffle the feathers on the fronts of her legs.

Being aware of these signs will be helpful if you plan to let Polly roam about the house. If you recognize your bird's body language when she's about to "go," you can quickly take her back to her cage or place her on a newspaper. The motion will frequently put a bird off-balance and give you a few critical extra seconds before things get messy.

I have one customer who holds his bird over the sink and says "Potty," and the bird will defecate in the sink. The man constantly rewarded his bird with praise or food after she dropped on cue, and now she is very good about cooperating in this sequence of events.

Birds, like some people, go to the bathroom when they are nervous. The more anxious they feel, the more frequently they go. Consider this carefully if you own a white sofa. If you are calmly watching television for an hour with your bird, she will likely wait until she returns to her cage before she makes any droppings. However, if your kids, your dog, and your spouse suddenly burst in the door and everyone becomes agitated, don't be surprised if a startled Polly leaves you a little present.

PASSIVE POLLY TURNS AGGRESSIVE

My bird has a very annoying habit of stamping his feet. Is he angry?

Birds who stamp their feet do it to show superiority. They are saying: "I'm the tallest bird in the flock. I'm looking for a mate. Look at *me!*"

Birds like to put on displays, sometimes to express a particular emotion, other times just to gain attention. Think about it: if a bird is performing, human beings are more likely to take an interest. Birds are no fools. They know this and will put on quite a show to solicit the attention of whoever is in the room.

Some baby conures will lie flat on their backs without moving. Sometimes I'll leave the store at night and see little feet sticking up in the air. The sight always causes me to pause and confirm that they are just comfortably sleeping on their backs. This action is just part of their nature, the way a cat might curl up into a ball or a dog might circle before lying down. Just check twice before hysterically calling the veterinarian to announce that your bird has died.

Like most pets, birds can be trained to behave in certain ways. In fact, given their proclivity for repetition and mimicry, they can often be taught very quickly. Birds can learn to stamp, lie down, jump up, and even roll over on command. If I put my macaw, Andy, in my lap and say "Dead bird," he will drop his head. I've trained him to do this by consistently rewarding him both vocally and with food, particularly the red grapes he loves so dearly. We have cockatiels who will climb quickly through a toilet paper tube if you put food at the other end.

A few bird owners attempt to train birds through food restriction; I find it's difficult to not let your buddy eat. If you want to train your bird to perform highly complicated routines and you choose this route, be certain to closely monitor the creature's weight.

Why does my bird pull on my mustache with his beak?

Polly is preening you. Preening is a meticulous and crucial task for birds. Their feathers consist of separate pieces that are attached to each other with Velcro-like parts. Polly draws her feathers through her beak and then zips them back together. This allows her to fly more efficiently, much the same way that pressing your fingers together helps you swim faster. In addition to zipping their feathers together, many pet birds oil their feathers with a slick substance from the uropygial gland, located at the base of the tail. They use their beaks to collect oil and then spread it across their feathers, essentially making a raincoat to protect them from dirt, water, and other substances.

Because you are a part of their flock, birds will preen you. They are fascinated by the defective feathers of your mustache, which are coarse and unzipped, and they will work diligently to correct the problem. Ticklish work. Birds will also style the hair on your head, if you let them. I don't advise allowing them to do this if you're headed out somewhere special for the evening or if you are a heavy user of hair spray.

CHAPTER 9

Embracing the Birdie Light:
Saying the final farewell

Life is eternal; and love is immortal; and death is only a horizon; and a horizon is nothing save the limit of our sight.

—ROSSITER WORTHINGTON RAYMOND,
"A COMMENDATORY PRAYER"

IT WAS 1989. WINTER WAS SLOWLY settling in, wrapping the East Coast in a blanket of chilly gray mornings and windy afternoons. Instead of taking to the city cafés and parks as they had a few months earlier, residents headed for the warmth of home and family after completing their day's work.

Susanna Gerber was one of them. A legal secretary for a prestigious Washington, D.C., law firm, at fifty-nine, Mrs. Gerber was one of the most meticulous workers at the office. She had never missed a deadline, and the company's partners depended on her for everything from keeping track of clients'

133

favorite wines to collecting obscure court rulings from across the country. At home, Mrs. Gerber and her husband lived a relatively modest existence. For nearly three decades they had resided in the same 1940s home located in one of Maryland's suburbs. In addition to her devoted work at the law firm, Mrs. Gerber maintained a clean, efficient home. Fresh flowers adorned the living room, the wooden floors shone, and any dust that settled on the windowsills rarely sat for long.

When they were first married thirty-two years earlier, the Gerbers bought a sulfur-crested cockatoo as a wedding present to each other. They named the bird Catherine after Mrs. Gerber's late mother, who had died a few years earlier. Catherine helped raise the Gerbers' two children, sitting on her perch patiently through years of schoolwork, adolescent tears, and young-adult dreams. Catherine kept Mr. Gerber company while he tinkered with workshop projects, calling out helpfully from her cage during the hammering and drilling. When the Gerbers went on vacation, Catherine either traveled with them in the car or stayed with close friends.

Most of all, Catherine loved to help Mrs. Gerber in the kitchen during meal preparation. No matter what the recipe, Catherine was always content to sit atop her cage watching the proceedings. Perhaps the bird was happiest there because she loved the sounds emanating from the various copper pots—Mrs. Gerber was a noteworthy chef—but more likely she relished sharing such a close bond with her owner.

Sometimes, after a particularly adventurous evening of cooking, Mrs. Gerber would leave Catherine's cage in the kitchen overnight. The kitchen was located next to their bedrooms, and more often than not, Mrs. Gerber would rise at some point in the predawn hours for a glass of water. She tiptoed so as not to wake Catherine, even though the bird was a particularly sound sleeper.

Given Mrs. Gerber's scrupulous attention to details, what transpired that January evening seems particularly unjust. After dinner with two close friends had run late, the Gerbers decided to clean the kitchen in the morning, rather than before bed, as was their usual practice. Catherine seemed content in the kitchen, and so Mrs. Gerber said good night to her before joining her husband in the next room.

At some point early the next morning—she could never recall the exact time—Mrs. Gerber awoke with a terrible headache. She put on her slippers and bathrobe and walked into the kitchen for a glass of water and some aspirin. Her steps were slow, and later she would remember that the furniture and walls leading to the kitchen seemed hazy. In the kitchen she flipped on a light. It took a moment for her eyes to adjust. She rubbed her temples and reached for a glass from the cupboard and filled it with water from the sink, staying quiet all the while so as not to disturb Catherine.

Just as she was about to cut off the light and return to her bedroom, Mrs. Gerber happened to glance at the birdcage, which was covered only with a lightweight white cloth because Catherine was such a heavy sleeper. She could barely discern the bird's outline under the cloth, but something seemed amiss. Instead of sitting upright, Catherine appeared to be on her side. At first Mrs. Gerber thought she was mistaken, perhaps because of the pain in her head. But she lifted the cover to check and saw Catherine lying in the oddest position and not moving at all. For a moment Mrs. Gerber stared at the lifeless bird, almost unbelieving. Then a small cry escaped from her lips and she went to wake her husband.

Embracing the Birdie Light *135*

The veterinarian at the animal hospital that morning was frank: Catherine had died of gas poisoning. Gas from the stove had somehow leaked into the Gerbers' house. If Mrs. Gerber hadn't discovered the bird when she did, both she and her husband could have been in grave danger.

A volunteer from the local fire department entered the Gerbers' home and discovered that the pilot light on the stove had gone out. The gas pipe was turned off until the Gerbers' house was fully aired out with open doors and windows. But none of that proved much consolation to the family. Although she could have done nothing to prevent Catherine's death, Mrs. Gerber blamed herself for leaving the bird in the kitchen that night. Moreover, she blamed herself for not having been more conscientious in making certain the pilot light was operating properly.

Losing a bird who has been in the family for a long time is especially devastating. I've known birds who have lived through three generations of a family. Even the smallest of parakeets can have a life expectancy of fifteen years or more, and that of larger birds can exceed one hundred years. One Amazon parrot whose toenails I trimmed still talked like Grandma, who had died two decades earlier. Indeed the bond between owner and bird may well have lasted longer than many human friendships and relationships.

HIDDEN HOUSEHOLD RISKS

No matter how careful the bird owner, many dangers lurk in the average home that can hurt and, in some cases, kill a bird.

Birds' respiratory systems are so sensitive that if there is a fire in the house, pet birds usually will die from the smoke before they can be rescued. In mines years ago, canaries were taken deep into the earth to monitor the safety of the air. If the bird died, the miners knew they had to evacuate the area. More recently, after the devastating gas episode in a Japanese subway, officers approaching the compound of the group responsible were pictured in full protective gear, carrying a bird in a cage.

Unfortunately many of the greatest dangers for birds aren't immediately obvious. Some types of glue, for example, can prove fatal. Young Roy kept two pet birds in his room. One Christmas morning his parents presented him with a complex model airplane kit. The boy became so absorbed in the project that he assembled the model in one afternoon, not noticing until it was too late that his yellow-collared macaw and his parakeet had both died from breathing fumes from the model glue.

Several types of nonstick pans have also been known to hurt birds. If the coating gets burned, the bird can inhale the fumes, which can kill him. Even if a birdcage is situated in another room, fumes emanating from the kitchen can inflict injury. If an exterminator comes to the house, make certain the bird isn't around. Many insect sprays will cause birds to become very ill and often to die.

If you live in an older home, the paint on your walls may contain lead, which can be fatal to birds who ingest it. Be careful where you place the cage. If it hangs near a spot where the paint is peeling, your bird might easily chew the toxic flakes. And if your bird is flying about the house, make certain he is under your watch at all times. Likewise, some antique birdcages can actually have lead in their seed-guard mesh: avoid these cages. And no matter how elegant an addition to your living room stained glass might be, the cames between the pieces of glass are made of lead and are dangerous for your birdie to chew on.

It's important to realize that birds are very adept at hiding their symptoms when sick. They instinctively do this because in a natural flock with other birds, any sign of weakness can lead the other members to take advantage of them.

Because they hide their symptoms, birds often fluff up their feathers to retain body heat while they are growing skinnier. Often this prevents their owners from noticing any gradual or even dramatic change in the bird's weight. Even worse, the owners sometimes think the bird is getting fatter because his fluffy feathers give that illusion. The owners think they need to cut back on their bird's food when the opposite approach is needed. Weight loss in a bird can be an indication of illness, in which case an astute owner will take the bird immediately to an avian veterinarian.

Weight loss is sometimes the fault of an inattentive owner. Perhaps the bird's tube feeder is clogged and no seeds are coming out. Or the problem could be something as simple as the owner's failure to realize that there are no seeds in the bird's dish—just empty shells. Remember that it only takes forty-eight hours for a tiny parakeet to starve to death when no food is available.

In addition to carefully feeling your bird and monitoring her food intake, you'll want to be aware of several signs of sickness to look for. Is the bird sitting on the floor of her cage instead of her perch, and is she moving about less than usual? This could be an indication that she isn't well and doesn't have the strength to climb onto her perch or reach her food and water. Does she refuse to take a bath or play with her toys? Has she stopped talking? If a noisy bird suddenly falls silent, perhaps you'll secretly be thankful, but you should also wonder about her health. Keep a close watch for any changes in your bird's behavior, particularly if she seems to have less energy than usual or isn't eating enough. How do you know if a bird is eating enough? Well, look at the droppings and see if they are consistent with the normal number and appearance.

Many people have called me to say, "But the bird was fine last night." They have no idea what has killed their pet. Many assume that Polly had a heart attack because her death appeared so sudden. Most often that is not the case. To keep Polly healthy, you must watch her health as closely as you would that of any other child in the family.

COPING WITH THE LOSS

Owners who lose a pet inevitably struggle with feelings of guilt. They know the creature was completely dependent upon them for survival. Even if the death was truly accidental, like that of Catherine, Mr. and Mrs. Gerber's cockatoo, the owners' first instinct is to blame themselves.

I've found that those owners who were actually negligent usually don't want to buy another pet. The day-to-day stress of caring for the animal proved too much for these people, and they aren't eager to jump into another relationship with the same responsibilities.

As with the death of people, all pet owners need time to grieve. With birds, customers frequently try to pick out another bird that looks almost identical to their recently deceased pet. Obviously, no two birds are the same. As we've explored in this book, bird personalities differ dramatically. Although it works in some situations, buying a bird that *looks* like Polly isn't usually the best move, because an owner will continually expect that bird to *act* like Polly.

Time for healing is the answer. How much time is a very individual decision. For children, the mourning process can be a lesson on how to deal with human death. They can learn about love and loss through their pets, which can be helpful preparation for the future. I've known parents who tried to replace their children's deceased bird with an identical clone and hoped the child wouldn't notice the swap. While this obviously is a personal decision, I can't say I encourage such techniques. First, a child can usually tell the difference. Moreover, a pet is as special as a person in many ways. Switching birds to avoid a child's tears hardly seems right or fair to anyone involved—human or animal.

THE BIRD'S MATE

There are other household members to consider after a bird's death, most notably the bird's avian partner or close friend. If a bird lived with another bird, whether in the same cage or not, the loss of a companion can be a very difficult adjustment for the survivor. He is accustomed to having a playmate at the very least, and sometimes the bond between actual mates who produce babies is even stronger.

The remedy for each bird is different, just as it is with people. I knew an Amazon parrot who lived with a plum-head parakeet named Willy. When Willy died, the other bird became extraordinarily depressed, quit playing, and started losing weight from not eating. The owner tried adding a new bird to the family but the Amazon did not respond. The owner grew increasingly concerned and finally came to Animal Exchange seeking advice. After hearing the problems, we recommended she buy another bird that looked similar to the deceased parakeet. She agreed and took a new plum-head parakeet home. The Amazon took one look at the bird and said, "Hello, Willy." They got along splendidly.

Other times, however, a replacement won't work. At a local senior citizens' home, the male parakeet died leaving his widow on her own. The seniors were very concerned about this turn of events, as was I. We decided the bird might like a new mate. So I put another male parakeet into the widow's cage. A few months later that male died. I tried a second bird. He too died a few months later. It wasn't until the third male replacement died within a year that the seniors finally decided the widow might prefer living alone. She wasn't attacking the male birds or killing them outright, but some birds can manipulate others in subtle ways. For instance, as the dominant member of the flock, the widow could have prevented the other bird from getting to its food supply. Or she might have bullied him into staying cramped in a particular part of the cage—probably not the highest perch, where she ruled supreme—thus limiting his ability to exercise. Whatever the case, it was clear that this female wanted to pass her remaining years in only the company of the seniors. Perhaps she could only love once.

STARTING OVER

Closing a chapter with one bird and beginning another with a stranger requires coming to terms with loss, much as it does with people. Frequently bird owners have invested significant time, energy, and heartache into training their bird. When the bird dies, they lose not only a pet but also a companion whose lifestyle—from eating and bathing to cooking and sleeping—meshed with their own. Deciding to try again is no small accomplishment.

So I was not surprised that three years passed after Catherine's death before the Gerbers were ready to acquire another bird. Susanna Gerber, particularly, was anguished about whether she was responsible for the cockatoo's death. She feared that another accident, like the leaking gas stove, might take the life of a new bird. For a long time the thought of incurring such a painful loss again was simply too much to bear.

But time heals. The Gerbers' children continued to raise birds, and around Christmas 1992, Mrs. Gerber came into the store seeking some toys and treats to put into tiny bird stockings for her kids' pets. She walked around slowly, looking at the plastic rings, ladders, and bells. For nearly twenty minutes she stayed far away from the clamor coming from the cages around her. I understood her reasons. The hurt from Catherine's death, I supposed, was still too strong. I applauded her for coming to the store at all.

Nearby, a new employee was feeding kale as a treat to a group of black-capped conures. While the birds' wings had been clipped, there had been enough new growth to enable some flight. As the employee opened the cage door and reached inside to hand the conures their food, one spritely young thing seized the opportunity and made a dash for the cage door. After slipping past the young man's hand, the bird charged into the open space of the store and, startled by its own courage, seemed suddenly uncertain about where to go.

Not far away, Mrs. Gerber was browsing in the birdseed section, her back turned to the small bird. Looking for a safe perch, the conure alighted on her shoulder with a tiny cry. Mrs. Gerber started, then slowly turned her head to look at the anxious creature resting on her shoulder.

Instead of brushing the bird off her shoulder, as I thought she might, Mrs. Gerber only gazed at him. As I watched from several feet away, her face softened and she spoke with the tenderness of a mother: "Yes, yes. What are you doing so far away from your cage? Silly little bird."

And as she whispered to him, she moved slowly across the room to his home. By the time she reached the cage, the bird appeared more relaxed. Mrs. Gerber tentatively reached up and offered her finger to the creature, who stepped aboard without hesitation. I watched from across the room as she just held him for a moment and looked into his alert face. He stared up at her, fluffed his feathers a bit, and then just sat still, making no motion to return to his cage.

She looked over at me, then back down at the bird. My heart quickened a bit when I heard her next words: "This little one, is he for sale?"

I told her yes, that little bird was most certainly for sale. They stood together a bit longer. She wanted to take him home, I could sense it, but she was scared. I knew Susanna Gerber was afraid the conure, like Catherine, would meet with a tragedy.

Finally I asked one of my employees to hold the baby conure. Then I put one hand on Mrs. Gerber's arm, guided her into my office, and shut the door behind us.

"You're frightened, aren't you?" I asked her. "You're worried that something terrible might happen to this little bird. Right?"

She looked down at her hands laced together in her lap and nodded slowly.

"Ruth, I couldn't bear to go through such grief again. Maybe I'm just not supposed to have another bird."

I smiled at her gently. "That's what we all think after a pet dies. But at some point we have to move on."

Mrs. Gerber shook her head, her eyes searching the walls of my office where yellowing posters of birds and other creatures hung. She was looking for clues, anything to give her a sign about what to do.

"Susanna, let me tell you a story," I said, leaning against my desk. "My father's favorite child, besides me, was a parakeet named Sampson. Dad loved that bird with all his heart, particularly because the Sampson was slightly handicapped. There was a problem with the bird's wings, and he couldn't fly at all. As a result, he spent a lot of time on the floor when he was out of the cage.

"But this only endeared him to Dad. Sampson also boasted a vocabulary of nearly fifty words, and my father was so proud that he would put a tape recorder on the floor to catch the parakeet's phrases. I can't tell you how many times he made Mother and me listen to Sampson saying, 'Hi. Sampson's a good bird. Very good bird. Kiss-kiss. I love you.' Dad had taught him these sayings, and he thought the bird's conversations were amazing. I'll admit we got weary of the bantering after a while, but we humored him and listened."

Mrs. Gerber managed a small smile, and I continued.

"One afternoon, however, our neighbor came to visit with her twin toddlers, and the children were playing on the floor. As I said, Sampson also spent a lot of time on the floor, and the twins were not well coached in bird safety. My father was watching the children and Sampson when one of the twins stepped back and accidentally crushed the bird.

"I had never seen my father cry until that day. He blamed himself. He thought he could have saved Sampson if he'd been more vigilant."

I paused and then said softly, "He felt just the way you feel about Catherine."

Mrs. Gerber nodded, her eyes beginning to soften.

"I didn't think my father would get over it. He vowed to never own another bird. I tried to tell him that he couldn't have controlled what the twins did, but he wouldn't believe me. Months went by, and Dad wouldn't speak of Sampson again because it hurt him so much.

"The household was a lonely, quiet place. Finally I couldn't stand it any longer, and one day I arrived at the house with a gray baby cockatiel. My father wasn't feeling well at the time; in fact he was perpetually tired in those days. When I arrived with the bird, he was too weak to protest. Instead, he just sat down in his easy chair and watched me play with the bird.

"Finally I made up some story about needing to help Mother in the kitchen and asked him to look after the cockatiel for a few minutes. A flicker of panic crossed his face— like the panic you're feeling now."

Mrs. Gerber's cheeks reddened a bit, but she kept listening. I looked out through the office window into the store at all the animals: guinea pigs, birds, snakes, fish, and even a chinchilla. They all deserved good homes, I thought. So did this little bird that had taken such a liking to Mrs. Gerber.

"Anyway, I left the bird on Dad's armchair and disappeared into the kitchen. They were alone for about fifteen minutes. I half expected to hear my father's deep voice hailing me to come and take the bird away, but he never called out to me.

"When I walked back into the room, Dad's eyes were closed and he was very still, but one finger was gently rubbing the bird's crested gray head. The bird didn't move when I entered; it just stayed on that armchair with Dad, as if such shared moments were routine. I watched them together a bit longer, and then I said good-bye to Mother, and I left."

Mrs. Gerber was watching me intently now. I leaned toward her. "My father and I never spoke about the little cockatiel again. The bird just stayed with Dad. My father named him Basie, for one of his favorite jazz musicians, Count Basie.

"Not long afterward my father got very sick. He was diagnosed with bladder cancer and went to the hospital for treatment every week. Sometimes he stayed for several days. Mother told me that she truly believed the one thing that inspired him to come home was the desire to see Basie. He was too weak by then even to read the newspaper. But that sweet tiny bird would push its head under his finger, and Dad could always summon the energy to rub the bird's neck until the cockatiel was happy.

"Basie outlived my father. Sometimes that's the way it happens. It wasn't the bird's fault that Dad finally lacked the strength to keep breathing. Just as it wasn't Dad's fault when that child crushed Sampson."

I paused again. "Just as it wasn't your fault that Catherine died.

"Susanna, little Basie needed a home where he could be happy and safe, just as Dad needed a new bird to bring him pleasure after Sampson died. Finding someone new didn't diminish the love he felt for Sampson. It simply meant he tucked his old feelings into a special protected place in the soul and then opened his heart to a new bird. It was the right thing to do."

Mrs. Gerber stood up and walked to the window and looked out at the baby conure, who was marching up and down my employee's arm. She smoothed her hair and took a deep breath. "Well," she began gently, "I suppose someone does need to give that little fellow a home. Otherwise he'll just get into trouble trying to dart out of his cage. He's a spirited one, you know. I can tell. I do believe we've got some space in the bedroom."

I nodded. Mrs. Gerber put her hand on the doorknob, twisted it halfway, and then turned around.

"Ruth," she said, "thank you."

Rarely do I have the time to contemplate why I love what I do for a living. Like most people, I suppose, I'm always just too busy to slow down and ponder why my work makes me happy. There is always a customer to help, a cage to clean, or a new shipment of pet supplies to sort through. Running Animal Exchange is a seven-day-a-week, twenty-four-hour-a-day commitment. I can't play hooky one morning because I'm tired. The well-being of hundreds of creatures rests in my hands. I simply cannot let them down.

But as we helped Mrs. Gerber pack up her new little conure that afternoon, I found myself strangely content and reflective. Experiences like hers were the reason I initially opened Animal Exchange. My mission was not merely to create a place where people could swap money for pets, as the name of my shop might suggest. No, I wanted this tiny outlet to become a hub where animals and humans could find each other, start a friendship, and then spend years sharing the love and tranquillity each had the power to give.

All of the animals we care for are lovely in their own way, but in my mind birds are the ones who most often allow me to fulfill my mission.

I keep nearly twenty birds at home, in a special room I've added to my house—the only room in my home with air-conditioning. And so many years after owning my first parakeet, I remain enamored of these charismatic creatures.

It isn't their flight that makes me love them, because I do not like to fly.

It isn't their music, because I am tone-deaf.

It isn't a need for commitment. I've raised three children and could do very well without waking up at 5:00 A.M. to feed and water these guys.

And goodness knows, birds can be imperious and hard to please. They can behave as if they've gone bonkers, and sometimes even the most valiant attempt on my part will not pacify them.

I forgive them.

I remember the wonder in the eyes of children when they first hear a parakeet speak. I recall the softened expression on the face of a senior citizen when a lovebird sits on his hand. I love the peep of a chick inside an unhatched egg. When I travel, sharing a hotel room with my birds makes the anonymity of the room disappear. And as I slide into my fifty-ninth year in this world, there is no voice I'd rather hear in the morning than the call of a peach-fronted conure who hopes I will wake up and join him.

I graduated from New York's Bronx High School of Science in 1956. In the class yearbook, beside my senior picture, is a quote. I have no idea who said the words, or when; it was such a long time ago. But the quotation reads like this:

"I was always a lover of soft winged things."

I still am.

About the Authors

Ruth Hanessian bought her first parakeet, Skippy, in 1949. She was ten years old. Since then she has owned more than one hundred birds and raised many of their babies. She opened Animal Exchange, a pet store, in Rockville, Maryland, in 1979. Over the years, Ruth has worked with the American Federation of Aviculture, which awarded her the Avy Award in 1977; the Pet Industry Joint Advisory Council; and the Maryland Association of Pet Industries, of which she is a former president. She teaches parrot psychology classes at Animal Exchange four times a year to help bird owners learn to cope with their pets' peculiarities.

Wendy Bounds, a staff reporter for *The Wall Street Journal,* lives in New York City. She is the daughter of a North Carolina veterinarian.